DEVELOPING LANGUAGE SKILLS:
Reading 2

Exploring
Prose, Plays, Poems

Sheila Freeman and Esther Munns

M

Macmillan Education

First published 1986

Published by
MACMILLAN EDUCATION LTD
Houndmills, Basingstoke, Hampshire RG21 2XS
and London
Companies and representatives
throughout the world

Designed by Linda Reed

Illustrations by Aneurin Edwards and Taurus Graphics

Printed in Hong Kong

British Library Cataloguing in Publication Data
Freeman, Sheila
Core reading.
2 : Exploring prose, plays, poems.
1. English language—Grammar—1950-
I. Title   II. Munns, Esther
428   PE1112
ISBN 0–333–39802–5

Contents

Preface

From the authors: to the student

Teachers who write course books face similar challenges to the ones encountered by the students who are asked to work from them.

Selected material and ideas have to be talked through and tried out in appropriate classroom situations, through a variety of activities which might include further discussion, reading, writing, drawing and drama. We decided to discard or adapt some of our ideas and original material in response to comments from students and their teachers. You will be involved in making the same kinds of decisions, from the earliest thoughts about your work to its final presentation in whatever form it takes. However, it is good practice to keep rough jottings, diagrams, first drafts and any other preparation material in a writer's notebook, not only for future reference but also as a record of how you set about organising your work.

For us, as joint authors, writing is seldom a solitary activity and is often accompanied by talk, both before we write and at helpful stages during the process of writing. You will have opportunities to experience both individual and collaborative note-making and writing, whichever is appropriate to the task. It is important to consider the audience for whom you are writing. Often it is your 'audience' which will help you to decide the form your writing should take; sometimes it is the material itself and your personal involvement with it which determines your choice of audience. We also believe that exploring literature through creative activities, role play and improvisation helps students to become more confident, independent thinkers and sensitive readers. We have chosen prose, play extracts and poems which should widen your reading experience and, at the same time, increase your understanding of the particular set texts you may be studying. As with writing and drama, reading is also a creative activity in which the reader is invited to enter into a partnership with the author. New meanings can be discovered and explored every time a piece of literature is shared. What you, as a student, have to contribute to the reading is your unique experience as a human being.

We hope that you will enjoy the opportunities that this book gives you to explore literature and language through a variety of ways of working. There is a 'shape' to the book; be guided by it. It is hoped, however, that you will enlarge upon what is offered by introducing 'yourself' to it — your thinking, talking, writing and reading 'self'.

1 Picking up clues

NOVEL

After the First Death, Robert Cormier

Are you still a free reader, or have you become a victim of the 'set book syndrome'?

It is the experience of publishers, librarians, booksellers and teachers that when students begin their study of 'set books' they are less likely to continue reading widely.

Our experience is that those students who do go on reading a wide range of literature, which might include newspapers, magazines, romances, horror stories, fantasy, science fiction and historical novels as well as non-fiction, find it easier to study selected books in depth. Just as we become better writers by writing, so we become better readers by reading.

Getting started on a book is often difficult, but we can reduce our uncertainties by making use of the clues available to us even before we begin to read.

Talking

For work in pairs or small groups.

On the following pages are the covers of two editions of the book *After the First Death* by Robert Cormier. All the other information reproduced here is taken from the 'prelim pages' of each edition.

Study *in detail* and talk about both covers and all the other information given. Appoint one person to take notes of the discussion. Remember to use *all* the clues provided in your attempts to predict what the story is about.

Prepare your comments and predictions for a general class discussion. Include questions which you expect the reading of the book to answer.

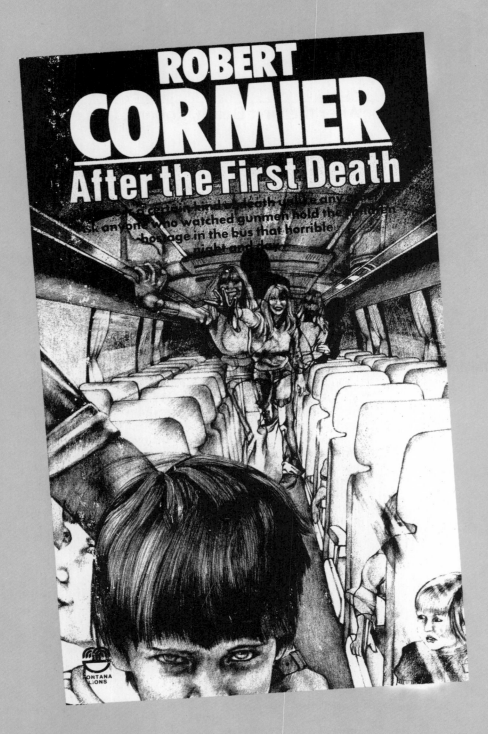

ROBERT
CORMIER
After the First Death

...a certain kind of death unlike any of...
...ask anyone who watched gunmen hold the children
hostage in the bus that horrible
night and day...

FONTANA
LIONS

ROBERT CORMIER

Robert Cormier's new thriller is set high on a bridge in Massachusetts, where a powerful drama of patriotism and daring unfolds, where ordinary people are forced to perform heroic acts, and the innocent play murderous roles:

A general who does not want to be a general.

A sixteen-year-old trigger-man anticipating his first kill.

A beautiful teenage girl forced to use a woman's weapons in a deadly game.

And the misfit son of the head of Inner Delta, a secret intelligence unit, who learns that it is possible to die more than once.

'A psychological thriller written in crackling prose. If any author in the field can challenge J.D. Salinger or William Golding, it is Robert Cormier.'
Newsweek

'A remarkable achievement, an exploration of character and motivation through one of the world's terrifying phenomena.'
New York Post

Cover illustration by Jane Faber

U.K. £1.25

0 00 671705 5

After the first death,
there is no other.
DYLAN THOMAS

General Editor: Aidan Chambers

AFTER THE FIRST DEATH

A terrorist gang hijacks a school bus and holds the children hostage on a bridge just outside the small American town where they live. Among the terrorists are sixteen-year-old Miro, and Artkin the idealist and murderer whom Miro worships. By mischance that day, the bus is driven by Kate, a brave young girl who has to find reserves of courage and cunning she never knew she possessed. Then there is Ben, a General's son, sent in as an innocent messenger by a father he cannot understand, and the General himself, like the terrorist Artkin, a patriot ready to destroy others for his cause. As the hijack reaches its terrible climax, Robert Cormier explores the difficult realities of loyalty and betrayal, courage and cowardice, patriotism and politics, love and hate. His novel is brilliantly written, almost hypnotic in its power to hold its readers, and profoundly important in what it has to say.

Robert Cormier is a much-admired American writer who lives in Massachusetts, where he works as a political journalist for a newspaper. He has written two other novels which are included in M Books: *The Chocolate War* and *I Am the Cheese*.

AFTER THE FIRST DEATH

A wave of terror sweeps a New England town when a school bus is seized by a group of masked men demanding a huge ransom, the release of political prisoners, and something more . . .

Inner Delta is the code name for a secret US Army counter-terrorist agency. Unless it is dismantled the children will die, one by one.

Out of this pressure-packed stalemate, Robert Cormier has woven a story of fathers and sons, nations and their secrets, loyalty and betrayal, seduction and sudden death, that is as timely as it is magnificently written.

'The book explores not only the nature of betrayal, but of courage. It exposes the evil inherent in patriotism. Violence and death occur; not just physically, but on the more subtle levels of emotion and thought. Nor is the morality simplistic. The terrorists do not wear baddies' black hats, nor the government white.'

Time Out

First published in the USA 1979
by Pantheon Books Inc
First published in Great Britain 1979
by Victor Gollancz Ltd
First published in Fontana Lions
by William Collins Sons & Co. Ltd
14 St James's Place, London SW1
Third Impression November 1982

Copyright © 1979 by Robert Cormier

Printed in Great Britain by
William Collins Sons & Co. Ltd, Glasgow

To my daughter RENÉE with love

To daughter RENÉE with love

© Robert Cormier 1979

First published in the USA by Pantheon Books Inc 1979
First published in Great Britain by Victor Gollancz 1979
Published in Fontana Lions 1979

First published in *M Books* 1983

Published by
MACMILLAN EDUCATION LIMITED
Houndmills Basingstoke Hampshire RG21 2XS
and London
Associated companies throughout the world

Printed in Hong Kong

Cover illustration by Young Artists/Philip Hood

Writing

Read the first page of the novel, reprinted below.

I keep thinking that I have a tunnel in my chest. The path the bullet took, burrowing through the flesh and sinew and whatever muscle the bullet encountered (I am not the macho-muscled type, not at five eleven and one hundred eighteen pounds). Anyway, the bullet went through my chest and out again. The wound has healed and there is no pain. The two ends of the tunnel are closed although there's a puckering of the skin at both ends of the tunnel. And a faint redness. The puckering has a distinct design, like the old vaccination scar on my father's arm. Years from now, the wound will probably hurt the way my father's old wounds hurt him, the wounds he received in those World War Two battles. My mother always jokes about the wounds: oh, not the wounds themselves but the fact that he professes to forecast weather by the phantom pains and throbbings in his arms and legs.

Will my wound ache like his when I am his age?

And will I be able to tell when the rain will fall by the pain whistling through the tunnel in my chest?

I am joking, of course, but my joking is entirely different from my mother's tender jokes.

I am joking because I won't have stayed around to become a human barometer or an instrument capable of forecasting weather.

But–who's the joke on?

The first of many questions about my presence here.

Keep a scorecard handy.

My father is scheduled to visit me today.

His first visit since the Bus and the Bridge last summer.

I am typing this in the room at Castle and it's beautiful here as I write this. Through the window, I can see the quadrangle...

■ Who do you think the 'I' is in the story? Give reasons for your guessing.
■ What do you learn about the narrator's state of mind from this short extract?
Now read the following extract from the middle of the book.

'Why are you doing this?' she asked, trying to keep any harshness out of her voice, needing to seem friendly and interested. By *this* she meant the bus, the children, the hijacking, this entire nightmare.

Miro knew her meaning. 'It's what we must do,' he answered in his carefully measured English, as if he were walking a verbal tightrope. 'Our work, our duty.'

'You mean your work is to kidnap children, hurt people, terrorize them?' The hell with trying to appear docile, let the chips fall.

'It's the war. It's all a part of the war.'

'I haven't heard of any war.'

He looked so young, so defenseless, the brown eyes innocent, the mouth sensitive. So unlike the person in the mask.

After Antibbe left the bus with one last lingering look at her, Kate had retired to the back seat and sat there, pondering the time ahead and what she must do. One of the things was winning Miro over. Or at least getting him to talk, to let down his defenses. She had seen that look in his eye and had to take advantage of what that look meant. He had to look upon her as a human being. More than that: as a desirable young woman, and not a victim. She knew the perfect terrible truth of the situation: she had to make it hard for him to kill her. Thus, when he looked her way on his return as he checked the children, she forced a smile to her lips. A weak substitute of a smile maybe, but it had done the trick. After a few moments, Miro came and sat beside her on the back seat. He removed his mask and placed it on the seat beside him.

And now they were talking about some kind of war, something she hadn't expected when she'd started this conversation. But, she thought: At least, we're talking, we're communicating.

'The war is going on all the time,' Miro continued. It was a topic he loved, a topic they had discussed much in the school. 'Our duty is to let the people know the war exists, that the world is involved in it, that no one is free from war until our homeland is free.' He wished Artkin was here to listen to him, to see how well he had learned his lessons.

'Where's your homeland?' Kate asked.

'My homeland is far from here. Across the ocean.'

Kate detected a wistfulness in his voice. 'What's its name?'

Miro hesitated. He had not said the word of his homeland for so long – like his own name – that he wondered how it would sound on his tongue. And he hesitated also because he did not know how much he should tell this girl. He wanted to win her confidence, but he must not betray himself or the others. If he did not say his name aloud to Artkin, how could he tell this girl the name of his homeland? 'You do not know the place,' Miro said. 'But it is a place of beauty.'

'Tell me about it,' Kate said.

'I have never been there. I have never seen my homeland.'

'You've never seen it?' Kate asked, incredulous. 'How do you know your homeland is so beautiful then and worth all – all this?'

'I have heard the old men talking in the camps and they have said how beautiful it is. They say that if you take off your shoes, you can feel the richness of the land on the skin of your feet. The orange trees are fruitful and the flight of the turtle dove and the lark is balm to the eyes and spirit.' He was quoting the old men now, and his voice was like music. 'The river there is gentle and the sun is a blessing on the earth and turns the flesh golden. The sky is the blue of shells washed by fresh rains.'

Kate thought: This strange, pathetic boy.

And then remembered that he carried a gun and one child had already died.

'Katie, Katie,' one of the children cried.

The cry brought back the reality of the bus, the heat, the oppressiveness, the plastic pail nearby that reeked of urine.

Kate listened, but the child did not cry out again.

'The old men in the camps,' Kate said. 'What camps?'

Miro was pleased with her question. She was becoming interested: he was doing his job well. But how could he tell her about the refugee camps, that endless string of filthy crowded places he and Aniel had drifted through in the early years of their lives, unknown and unwanted in a terrible kind of anonymity? They had existed on the generosity of strangers, and when they did not encounter generosity, they stole. Aniel was the expert at theft. Sometimes Miro acted as a decoy in the makeshift marketplaces, while Aniel's swift hands grabbed and clutched whatever was at hand. Nothing was ever useless. You made use of whatever came your way. Even the time Aniel had wrenched a battery from an old abandoned truck. They had bartered it for food. The food was spoiled and sickened them. But then the battery was also useless. How could he tell the girl all this?

'My people are outcasts, our homeland occupied by others. But we were allowed to live in camps,' Miro said, wanting to hold her interest without telling her about the hunger and the stealing and the begging. He did not want to diminish himself in her eyes.

'You said *we,*' Kate said. 'Who was *we*? Your family, your parents?'

'Only my brother Aniel and me. He was two years older.'

'How about your parents?'

He translated the American word *parents* into the word for mother and father in the old language and tried at the same time to summon feeling, emotion, *something*, but could not.

'I never knew my father,' Miro said. 'I never knew my mother.' For some reason, he always felt guilty about this: not knowing his parents, having no remembrance of them. Why did he feel guilty? He pondered this in the small hours of the night when sleep did not come. Do not waste your time with the past, Artkin had told him once. The past is gone; the present is enough. And the future will bring us back our homeland. He had said to Artkin: 'My father and my mother are in the past, and if I don't remember them, who will?' And Artkin had turned away without an answer. So Artkin did not know everything, after all.

Now, Miro said to the girl, 'I have no memory of them.'

There was a strange expression on her face. What was it? Sadness? No. He would have treated a sad look from her with contempt. He did not want her sadness. The look told of something else but he could not name it. A strangeness in her eyes as if in a moment she would either burst forth with laughter or dissolve in tears. He was confused. No one had ever looked at him with such – such intimacy before. And to cover his confusion, he found himself telling her:

'In those days, there were always attacks on the border. And there were times when we did not know who was enemy or friend. Mines were planted in the gardens. Cattle was slaughtered in border raids. Planes dropped bombs or raked the earth with machine-gun fire. Homes were burned. Aniel said that our father and mother were blown up by a mine planted in our garden. Someone told him this. But Aniel also said: "Let us not talk about it. They are alive in us. As long as we are alive, one of us, then they will never be dead." And now Aniel is dead.'

'I'm sorry,' she said. And he looked at her again. For signs of – he did not know what. She was only a girl, an American at that, and she meant nothing to him outside of the fact that she was his victim, his first death. She should have been dead hours ago. She would be dead hours from now. By his hand. His gun. Who was she to say *I'm sorry*? Only those most intimate should say words like that. Even Artkin had not said them, but had turned away in respect.

Kate sensed that she was losing him, that she had said something to turn him off. He had been so open one moment and then his faced had closed her out, his eyes dropping away. Maybe it hurt him to talk about his parents and his dead brother. Maybe her instincts were correct, after all, and she was on the right track: he was vulnerable, sensitive. She couldn't lose him now. Instinctively, she turned to the oldest weapon she knew, remembering how it had never failed her.

'You speak English beautifully,' she said, flattering him . . .

■ What differences in style and viewpoint do you notice?
■ What links in the story can you make between page 1 and the middle pages? Remember to make use of your previous talk and any other predictions you have already made.
■ What do you learn about Kate and Miro from this extract which might help you to anticipate what happens next?

Drama

In this extract Kate is forced to change her first impression of Miro when he removes his *mask* and becomes a *face*.

In pairs

Read aloud only the dialogue between Kate and Miro. Pick up the clues from the narrative to help you to decide how to read your parts.

Scripting dialogue

Begin by setting the scene. In order to do this you will have to look closely at the paragraph beginning, 'After Antibbe left the bus . . .'

Use the narrative to write instructions (keep them brief and few) to help your actor and actress to interpret their characters. Sometimes the clues you need will appear before the dialogue you are scripting; sometimes they will be found immediately following and occasionally much later, e.g.

'Where's your homeland?' Kate asked.
'My homeland is far from here. Across the ocean.'
Kate detected a wistfulness in his voice. 'What's its name?'
Miro hesitated . . .

might be written in play form as:

KATE   [*trying to win Miro over*] Where's your homeland?
MIRO   [*wistfully*] My homeland is far from here. Across the ocean.
KATE   [*quietly*] What's its name? [*Miro hesitates*]
MIRO   [*cautiously*] You do not know the place. [*pause*] But it is a place of beauty.

It is likely that you will overdo the instructions to the actors on your first draft and may need to cut out some of them if the dialogue 'speaks' for itself.

Prepare your dialogue for sharing with another pair. Share your work. Note any differences in interpretation and decide where you need to make any changes.

Before you decide to read the whole book you might like to continue the dialogue, bringing it to a point at which you leave the audience wondering what is going to happen next.

Improvisation

In pairs, imagine that two characters, faced with a threatening situation, are forced to change their first impressions of each other because of the time they spend together in which they discover 'a face behind a mask', e.g. two people arrive for an interview for the same job.

During your reading of plays you will discover many examples of ways in which characters change their views of each other during the development of the plot, e.g. Bamforth in *The Long and the Short and the Tall* comes to recognise the Japanese soldier as a fellow human being.

As readers we are constantly being required to reassess our thoughts and feelings about characters as we learn more about them.

Don't make a distinction between the way in which you approach your free reading and your 'set books'. Before you start to read, pick up the clues and be prepared to guess your way into the book, play or poem.

Further reading

When Robert Cormier visited London, some fourth year students who talked to him learned something about the background to his novels for young adults and about his approach to writing. Part of that interview is included here in the hope that you will be encouraged to read his other books as well as *After The First Death*.

About *The Chocolate War*: Are schools really as violent as that in America?

No, not really it's because there aren't people like Archie in a great many schools. The potential is always there though for violence of one kind or another. I've always thought that there was more psychological violence in the book. The physical encounters are almost controlled, but it's the intimidation that I think is more evident than any physical violence.

When the book first came there was some criticism that it sounded like an attack on the Catholic school system, and they said why didn't you just make it any school. The reason why I didn't is I think an author should be specific for reasons of truth – otherwise you end up compromising and end up with something bland like milk. I figured that I would be specific, hoping that the reader would see that there are Archies everywhere, there are headmasters like Brother Leon everywhere, not only in schools but in business. I was using this school as a metaphor for life, a chance to dramatize the little but deadly things which go on among people all the time.

My son went to a school very similar to this school and there was a chocolate sale there – it didn't turn out to be a war, it was a skirmish. And in fact my son didn't sell the chocolates. We talked about it at home and just left the option to him. He said I really feel I don't want to sell the chocolates. I wrote a letter to his headmaster showing that he wasn't doing this frivolously but out of principle. He presented the letter to the headmaster who kind of gulped and got a little red and said 'fine'. Nothing happened; the sale went on, the school is still there, there was no intimidation. But then I began to think – using the two words that I think all writers use – 'what if?' What if the headmaster had been unscrupulous and ambitious and what if chocolate sales were very important, not just another event? And what if there were peer pressure? And these were things I wanted to explore: the do-your-own-thing philosophy, whether people really mean it, and the individual fighting a system, and I began writing from that point and let things follow what I call a sense of inevitability. Once these forces were set in motion I just followed through with it.

Was the book written specially for young people?

No, it was written really for any age-group. In fact I'd written three previous novels, early in the 60's, and when I began writing this I described the story over the phone to my agent and immediately she said it sounds like a young adult novel, immediately scaring the daylights out of me because I thought I'd have to go back and simplify. She said just write the novel as you would because the young adults of today are capable of reading a novel without being written down to. It was published as a young adult novel but the publisher also sold it on an adult level at the same time.

Why do you think your books are so different from many other books for teenagers – more serious and more violent?

When I wrote *The Chocolate War* I didn't know what other people were writing for young people, so I didn't feel I was departing from what they were doing. I was just writing in my own way. I've read some of the other books now, and I'd say a lot of the newer writers in the last few years are tackling themes that weren't being written about ten years ago – not only violence but other things in our society. I think just about any theme is workable if it's written seriously and in good taste, but not diluted to the point where it's not effective. I think you have to have a certain amount of realism – but never gratuitously or never only for effect, but to have a place. The language in *The Chocolate War*, for example: it's an outspoken novel, but once I established that boys talked like this I didn't wallow in it, I tried to let up a little because I didn't want the language to get in the place of the story I was trying to tell. Or too much violence. And yet I thought there were certain things that had to be in there. I try for what I call the shocks of recognition, to have people read it and say, 'yes that's the way it is', or 'that's the way it was for me'. It's always a matter of selection; an author is constantly making choices: shall I do it this way or that way?

The freshest example for me is in *After the First Death*. There's a scene in which a girl had hidden a key and her captors found out that she had hidden it. She had to be searched. Now it would have been one thing to have had the teenage boy, Miro, search her: this would have been a sensitive and sensational thing, but I felt that it wasn't right for the book and that this other man, who would do it very impersonally, should do it. I chose the way it should be rather than the more exciting way. And at the end of *The Chocolate War* I would have loved to have had Jerry win the day or to have the other colour marble come out of the hat – and at one time I thought that might happen and yet when I got to that point events just seemed to dictate the way it did end.

What about your later book, *After the First Death*?

Well the title comes from Dylan Thomas: 'After the first death there is no other'. Actually for a while I was thinking of using the word 'Orange' as the title. 'Orange' is one of the few words in the language for which there is no rhyme. Originally I had one of the hijackers in the book say to another how they are outcasts, how they are like the word 'orange' because no-one rhymes with us. And then I took this out, and then discarded the title principally because I didn't want people to think 'chocolate . . . cheese . . . orange' and think I had some kind of food fetish.

The book explores the various kinds of deaths, not only physical deaths – hopefully it does that anyway. And again the story came together from two things that were bothering me, I live in a small town right outside of an army installation – and there's a secret agency there. This to me has always been a brooding presence right in the middle of this lovely New England landscape. So I've always wanted to explore that and you know you read about terrorist attacks and they always seem to happen elsewhere, and then I thought suppose it happened here: what would be the reaction? And the inevitable link was with the army installation. I've always wanted to explore how patriotism can be perverted and how innocence can become evil.

VERSE

How to read a poem

The study of poetry in the classroom has long been regarded as a problem area for both teachers and their pupils. It is difficult to understand why this should be since young children delight in a natural sense of rhythm and show a willingness to engage in playground and word games, jingles and nursery rhymes. They certainly seem to accept writing verse as a natural form of expression; they love poems being read to them and choose a poetry book as freely as a story book. Some of the reasons why poetry ceases to be enjoyed by older students in the secondary school might be its association with comprehension exercises, test situations and a notion that poetry is too remote in subject matter and too difficult for 'ordinary' people to appreciate. There is no doubt that the 'teaching' rather than the 'sharing' of poetry has led to many unhappy and frustrating experiences for those involved.

Making poetry accessible to young people has occupied the minds of many poets and teachers during the last few years. Instead of 'cracking the code', of guessing what is in the teacher's head when answering questions based on a poem, a more positive and imaginative way of working might be to try the approach suggested by Richard Exton in an article called 'The Language of Literature'.

How to read a poem – a guide in ten easy steps

If possible, follow this guide with one or two friends. If you do, talk about all the possibilities before you write anything down.

STEP 1   Forget about what the poem may or may not mean, or what it may be about.

STEP 2   Look at the title and jot down about half a dozen things that it suggests to you. Give literal meanings as well as associations.

STEP 3   Read the poem once quickly and then three times very slowly. Try to hear the poem aloud in your head.

STEP 4   Make a list of all those things which force their attention on you or which catch your interest for one reason or another. You might jot down unusual/odd/ striking

words or striking rhymes or repetitions or patterns or
contrasts or echoes, etc. etc.

STEP 5 Look at and list any features of the language used in the
poem, e.g.
No capital letters
No full stops at line-ends
Presence/absence of adverbs/adjectives
All verbs active/passive
Tense – all past until last line, etc.

STEP 6 Try to find groups of words (thematic boxes) e.g.
(a) All similes make reference to animals/death/plants,
etc.
(b) All the first words of lines are conjunctions, etc.
N.B. Don't worry if your groups of words seem silly or
improbable.

STEP 7 Look at your lists, notes and groups. Do you see any
pattern taking shape? Try out a few.

STEP 8 Read the poem again and then try out a few hunches
about what the poem may mean.

STEP 9 Answer the following questions
(a) Who is 'speaking' the poem?
Is it the poet or has s/he invented someone or
something to speak through?
(b) Who is the poem 'spoken' to?
Is it to a particular person or to the poet him/herself
or to the public in general?
(c) What is the speaker's attitude to that audience? Is it
angry, sincere, jokey, teasing?
(d) What is the poet's attitude to his/her audience?
(e) Why is the poem organised in the way it is?
(f) What is the effect of all the things you have noted at
Steps 2, 4, 5 and 6?

STEP 10 Now, if you wish to, or *have to* (because of an exam) you
can write a critical appreciation of that poem.

We asked one fifth year group to read the following poem by
D.H. Lawrence and then to respond to steps 2, 4, 5 and 6 of
Richard Exton's guide. First the poem:

Discord in Childhood

Outside the house an ash-tree hung its terrible whips,
And at night when the wind rose, the lash of the tree
Shrieked and slashed the wind, as a ship's
Weird rigging in a storm shrieks hideously.

Within the house two voices arose, a slender lash
Whistling she-delirious rage, and the dreadful sound
Of a male thong booming and bruising, until it had drowned
The other voice in a silence of blood, 'neath the noise of the ash.

Then their response:

Step 2 – consideration of title
argument in childhood
unhappiness, argument, fear
mother, music
lack of harmony
broken friendship
separation of parents
divorce

Step 4 – words/phrases of interest
terrible whips
weird rigging
slender lash
she-delirious
male thong
booming and bruising
silence of blood

Step 5 – language
2 sentences
one sentence to each verse
run on lines
rhyme: 1st and 3rd line
       2nd and 4th line
       5th and 8th line
       6th and 7th line

Step 6 – structural
boxes

whips, lash
slashed, shrieks
thong

male
female
discord in childhood

outside
inside

noise
silence

ash tree
lash of *tree*
noise of *ash*

shrieked/slashed
booming/bruising

Talking and writing

Work in small groups.
■ Are there any other possibilities that you would like to add to those already suggested?

- Work through steps 7, 8, 9 and 10.
- Share your thoughts about this poem with other groups.
- Choose another poem from this or any other book and explore it using the guidelines.

'Thirty-six things to do with a poem'

This was the title given to a list of ideas for the teaching of poetry compiled by a group of teachers at an annual conference of the National Association for the Teaching of English.

Eight of the ideas, which are of special interest to older students, are:

1   Two pupils write brief 'instant reaction' comments about a poem and exchange them. Add a comment on each other's responses before discussion.

2   Pairs or groups are presented with a poem with particular words omitted and asked to speculate about what might best fit in.

If specific words are omitted the group's attention can be focused on particular aspects of the poem – its imagery, rhyme or rhythm, for example, as well as its diction.

Here is a poem by Elizabeth Jennings from which certain words have been omitted.

My Grandmother

She kept an antique shop – or it kept her.
Among Apostle spoons and Bristol glass,
The _____ silks, the heavy _____
She watched her own reflection in the_____
Salvers and _____ bowls, as if to prove
Polish was all, there was no need of_____

And I remembered how I once refused
To go out with her, since I was afraid.
It was perhaps a wish not to be used
Like antique objects. Though she never said
That she was hurt, I still could feel the guilt
Of that refusal, guessing how she felt.

Later, too _____ to keep a shop, she put
All her best things in one long _____ room.
The place smelt _____, of things too long kept shut,
The _____ of absences where _____ come
That can't be polished. There was nothing then
To give her own _____ back again.

And when she died I felt no grief at all,
Only the guilt of what I once refused.
I walked into her room among the tall
Sideboards and cupboards – things she never used
But needed; and no finger-marks were there,
Only the new dust falling through the air.

Reading and talking

Read the poem aloud – you could say the word 'something' where there is a blank.

Discuss what the completion possibilities are, picking up your clues from verses two and four and keeping in mind the following considerations.

■ *Sense* within the line, as well as within the poem as a whole.
■ *Grammatical* fit.
■ *Rhythm*: ten syllables to each line.
■ *Rhyme*.
■ *Repetition*.
■ *Assonance* i.e. repetition of vowel sounds as in 'give', 'miss' and 'guilt'.
■ *Alliteration* i.e. repetition of the same consonant sound.

Jot down your suggestions and then compare your reconstruction with the original. A list of deleted words is given on page 22.

3 A poem is given to a class untitled. In pairs they propose titles, leading possibly to consensus. Compare with the poet's title.

4 Pairs or groups are presented with a poem in segments to be placed in what they judge to be the best order. This is then compared with the full text of the poem.

Talking and writing

The following list is made up of twenty-one scrambled segments from a poem by C. Day Lewis. Some clues have been provided to help you rearrange them.

A Next you appear
   As if garlands of wild felicity crowned you –
B Has blossomed again,' she murmurs, 'all that you missed
   there
   Has grown to be yours.'
C Listening as if beguiled
   By a fancy beyond your years and the flowering maytime.
D I cry: 'Give not to those charming desperadoes
   What was made to be mine.'
E The last. It would show me a tree stripped bare
F The answer she finds in that oracle stream
   Only time could affirm or disprove.
G The print is faded: soon there will be
   No trace of that pose enthralling,
H By intemperate gales, her amazing

Noonday of blossom spoilt which promised so fair.
I Yet, scanning those scenes at your heyday taken,
   I tremble, as one who must view
J Courted, caressed, you wear
   Like immortelles the lovers and friends around you.
K One picture is missing –
L Then I turn the page
   To a girl who stands like a questioning iris
M Then I see her, petalled in new-blown hours,
   Beside me — 'All you love most there
N 'They will not last you, rain or shine,
   They are but straws and shadows,'
O In the crystal a doom he could never deflect – yes, I too
   Am fruitlessly shaken.
P I close the book;
   But the past slides out of its leaves to haunt me
Q I see you, a child
   in a garden sheltered for buds and playtime,
R Yet I wish I was there to venture a warning, 'Love
   Is not what you dream.'
S And it seems, wherever I look,
   Phantoms of irreclaimable happiness taunt me.
T By the waterside, at an age
   That asks every mirror to tell what the heart's desire is.
U Nor visible echo of my voice distantly calling
   'Wait! Wait for me!'

Clues

The poem is in five stanzas of eight lines each. It tells how the lover, now old, has watched the beautiful girl he still loves, grow up. He recounts sadly how she had many lovers and was finally destroyed by them.

The title, *The Album*, is an important clue which should help you.

After working for some time, if you need a further clue, turn to page 22.

When you have finished reassembling the poem, turn to page 22 and look at what C. Day Lewis wrote. Jot down:
■ any discrepancies between your draft and that of the poet;
■ what you can remember about your method of working through the poem;
■ which clues helped you most;
■ what you have learned from working in this way.

5 Pupils make a picture which illustrates or captures the essence of the poem.

6 Pupils rework a poem in a different genre (e.g. as a newspaper item). What has been gained and what lost?

7 Groups prepare both factual and open-ended questions about the poem for other groups to answer.

8 Groups prepare a list of questions about a poem which they would like to ask their teacher.

Choose any of these suggestions which you feel would help you to a deeper understanding and enjoyment of the poem you are studying.

When you have read a great many poems, you might like to prepare a programme called 'Desert Island Poems', i.e. a group or a pair (subject and interviewer) prepare a list of, say, five favourite poems, with readings and reasons for selection.

Solutions

Words deleted from the poem, *My Grandmother* (p. 19):
faded, furniture, brass, silver, love, frail, narrow, old, smell, shadows, reflection.

Further clue to *The Album*:
The rhyme scheme of this poem is: *A B A B C D D C*

The poem by C. Day Lewis:

The Album

I see you, a child
in a garden sheltered for buds and playtime,
Listening as if beguiled
By a fancy beyond your years and the flowering maytime.
The print is faded: soon there will be
No trace of that pose enthralling,
Nor visible echo of my voice distantly calling
'Wait! Wait for me!'

Then I turn the page
To a girl who stands like a questioning iris
By the waterside, at an age
That asks every mirror to tell what the heart's desire is.
The answer she finds in that oracle stream
Only time could affirm or disprove,
Yet I wish I was there to venture a warning, 'Love
Is not what you dream.'

Next you appear
As if garlands of wild felicity crowned you –
Courted, caressed, you wear
Like immortelles the lovers and friends around you.
'They will not last you, rain or shine,
They are but straws and shadows,'
I cry: 'Give not to those charming desperadoes
What was made to be mine.'

One picture is missing –
The last. It would show me a tree stripped bare
By intemperate gales, her amazing
Noonday of blossom spoilt which promised so fair.
Yet, scanning those scenes at your heyday taken,
I tremble, as one who must view
In the crystal a doom he could never deflect – yes, I too
Am fruitlessly shaken.

I close the book;
But the past slides out of its leaves to haunt me
And it seems, wherever I look,
Phantoms of irreclaimable happiness taunt me.
Then I see her, petalled in new-blown hours,
Beside me – 'All you love most there
Has blossomed again,' she murmurs, 'all that you missed there
Has grown to be yours.'

DRAMA

The Queen and the Rebels, Ugo Betti

Plays are written to be performed in theatres, pubs, parks, village halls, schools or anywhere in which there is a space for players to act and an audience to participate.

We can best enjoy, understand and appreciate the 'play form' by taking every opportunity to see and to be involved in 'live' theatre.

Whether you are studying a play as an examination student or as an actress/actor preparing for a part in it, you will need to become skilled at seeing the text in theatrical terms and in picking up clues which help you towards a deeper understanding of characters and situations.

We asked an actor friend how he set about preparing to play a character part. Here is part of the letter he wrote in reply:

> I have occasionally been asked how I go about working on a character and usually say that I learn the lines as fast as possible and try not to bump into the furniture. But actually, on closer examination, what I think I really do is to approach a role rather as a detective investigates a case — that is, I search the text for clues. Who is he? How old? Where does he come from? What is his class and status? What are his attitudes and relationships with other characters? Often, the

best clues come from what other characters say about one — that is if their opinion is to be trusted.

In the case of a classic role, Hamlet for example, there's a whole lot of detective work that has already been done by scholars through the ages and one simply reads these works and sifts out what may be of use to the particular production. I must add, of course, that this shouldn't be done in isolation. One works closely with one's director and provided he's good at his job, he too will have done a lot of research. Also fellow actors are a great help and occasionally it may be worth getting together and improvising a scene when in difficulty.

The main thing is, whatever one does, however one chooses to play a part, it must be real. Even if a role is eccentric or farcical it must be based on truth — what people really do in life. All actors must study people in their daily business — the pomposity, the fears, loves, greeds etc. In fact, 'hold the mirror up to nature' as Shakespeare, who got it right about so many things, said.

Play reading, unlike the reading of a novel, is a difficult activity to undertake by yourself. Throughout your fourth and fifth year courses in English and Drama, you will have opportunities to work in groups and to have the benefit of everyone's ideas and expertise. This way of working will help you:
■ to become a better 'detective';
■ to use improvisation to explore meaning, characterisation and themes;
■ to conduct research into the period in which a play is set;
■ to study a play text that you might not have seen before.
We have chosen an extract from *The Queen and the Rebels* by Ugo Betti for you to explore after you have read the following short introduction.

The entire action of the play takes place from sunset to sunrise in a large hall in the main public building in a frontier village somewhere in Europe. Some five years before, a revolutionary group, the Unitary Party, had overthrown the monarchy and seized power. Not only did they shoot the royal family, they proceeded to wipe out all traces of the previous regime. In order to maintain their hold on the situation they introduced a secret police, censorship of ideas and firm control over the movement of people. Despite all this, a legend spread that the Queen, Elisabetta, had escaped the shooting and was in hiding.

The play begins with the revolutionaries fearing that their opponents might form a counter-revolutionary group with the Queen as their leader. It is rumoured that she is in the vicinity and tension is high.

Reading

Working in groups, read aloud the extract in which the revolutionaries, Amos (commissar), Biante (general) and Raim (interpreter), interrogate Argia, a traveller.

A number of peasants, men and women, have entered. The Engineer (a traveller) is among them.

BIANTE   [*to the newcomers*] Come in, my friends! Sit down. You already know that I have taken over the command. That means that everybody can kill a man, but I can do it with a roll of drums, like an acrobat making a difficult leap. The republic has conquered. [*He beats his fist on the table.*] Well then, I preside! [*To* AMOS] You shall be the accuser! [*To* RAIM] You shall write. [*To the newcomers.*] You shall judge! [*Lowering his voice.*] And after that, I, as president, if I'm still alive, shall carry out the sentence. You can begin, Amos.
[AMOS *has already risen: he speaks in the tones of a chancellor reading out an act.*]

AMOS   The accusation charges this woman with having concealed her identity, and falsified her papers.

ARGIA   Gentlemen! Please, please listen to me. I came up here . . .

AMOS   . . . with the intention of fleeing the country? Or to try to discover the whereabouts of your son? Yes, madam, we are fully informed about that also. Your son. [*His voice slightly rising.*] She is also accused of having formerly exercised a secret and illicit influence on the heads of the state, inducing them to enact factious and oppressive laws . . .

BIANTE   Oh, get on with it, Amos! You're cold, you've got no guts! You're just being cruel!

AMOS   [*louder*] . . . of inciting to massacre and persecution . . .

ARGIA   But I have never done anything of the kind!

AMOS   . . . of having fomented conspiracies aimed at undermining the authority of the State . . .

ARGIA   But that's what you've done! And you blame it on the Queen! *You* were the sowers of discord.

AMOS   [*louder*] . . . to the point of inducing a number of fanatics to take up arms against their country.

ARGIA   But I . . .

AMOS   This woman is accused of having herself unloosed the present conflict; of having herself driven it to atrocious excesses.

She herself summoned to this country foreign armed forces, herself lit the fires that now smoke from every point of the horizon, herself disfigured the dead along the roads . . .

AGRIA   But I tell you I . . .

AMOS   . . . didn't know? Didn't want it?

ARGIA   I tell you that my hands . . .

AMOS   Are clean? Is that it? That only shows how cunning you've been. It deprives you of extenuating circumstances, if there ever were any.

THE ENGINEER   [*suddenly and violently*] I was walking in the street one day: there was a cordon of soldiers; and they said to me: 'Not this way, the Queen will be coming down here.' I went round another way, and they told me: 'You can't come through here.' Everywhere I went, it was the same. Madam, you were always in the way.

ARGIA   Friends, friends, but I was there too, with you: on your side of the cordon, not the other.

A PEASANT-WOMAN   [*suddenly bursting into sobs*] The shirt I washed for my son, he said it was shabby. He said the soup I cooked for him tasted nasty. And now they've told me that he's lying out there, in the fields, with his arms wide-open, covered with ants. It's all the Queen's fault.

ARGIA   You stone that woman now, only because you one day fawned on her!

A PEASANT   [*violently*] When our children are old enough to play games, they're not allowed to play the same games as rich men's children. That's a terrible thing! That's what poisons their minds!

A PEASANT-WOMAN   My son hated the earthen crockery, he hated the smell of our home; he hated his own life!

A PEASANT   My daughter went away with the soldiers, and I haven't heard a word of her since. That was your fault!

A PEASANT-WOMAN   It was your fault!

BIANTE   All of you! All of you! Bear witness, all of you!

THE ENGINEER   It was her fault!

MAUPA   It was her fault!

OTHERS   Her fault! It was her fault!

BIANTE   And what about you? That porter over there! Are you the only one with nothing to say?
[*A silence.*]

THE PORTER   Yes . . . everything she did . . . humiliated us.

ARGIA   [*rebelliously, to the* PORTER] And who was it who taught you humiliation and envy? Who was it who let your rancour loose?

AMOS   [*with sudden intensity*] You, the apex of privilege, the symbol of prerogative; you, the emblem of those distinctions from which humiliation and rivalry were born. Your whole authority is based and built upon inequality. It is in you that injustice is personified, it is in you she finds her arrogant features, her scornful voice, her contemptuous answers, her sumptuous clothes, and her unsoiled hands. Your name of Queen is of itself enough to make men see that they are

unequal: on one side vast revenues, on the other, vast burdens.
You are the hook from which the great act of tyranny hangs.
The world will be a less unhappy place when you have
vanished from it.

ARGIA [*remains for a long moment with her head bent*] Forgive me. I
have been play-acting a little: perhaps too much. Now I will
tell you the truth. I can prove that I am not the Queen, and I
can prove it at once. There is someone here who can witness for
me.

BIANTE Who is it?

ARGIA That man over there, your interpreter, Stop, Raim, don't
run away. He knows me only too well. He knows I'm not a
queen. I'm the sort of woman who has to smile at lodging-
house keepers, and traffic in pawn-tickets.

RAIM [*comes forward slowly, in silence*] There must be some
misunderstanding. This woman must be mad. I've never seen
her before in my life.

ARGIA Look at me, Raim.

RAIM I am looking at you. [*To* AMOS.] I've never seen her before.

ARGIA [*turning to the others*] My friend is frightened things may
have gone too far. Whether I'm the Queen or not, or he's my
friend or not, he's afraid you just have to have a certain
number of people to shoot, up here. He just wants to stay alive,
that's all.

RAIM I knew you'd say that. But I must insist that I do not know
you.

ARGIA Gentlemen! I and this man, who 'doesn't know' me, kept
each other warm all through one whole winter!

RAIM Rubbish!

ARGIA I came up here solely to look for him. There are people
here who saw us talking.

RAIM [*to the others*] Of course they did. I tried to approach her:
because I thought she looked suspicious. I don't know who she
is. I'm sorry, madam, but I can't help you.
[*He moves away, disappearing among the others.* ARGIA *stands for a
moment in silence.*]

ARGIA [*almost absently*] Perhaps it's true. Perhaps that man and I
never did know one another. But, even so, gentlemen, that
doesn't give you the right to make stupid mistakes. If you have
to have a corpse to show people, when you tell them the
Queen's dead, you might at least look for a corpse a bit more
like her. You fools! I, the Queen? Is mine the voice of a queen
. . .? Has my life been the life of a queen . . .? [*Suddenly calling.*]
Raim! Raim! Call him back!

AMOS I'd like to bet that your friend is far away by now; and
making for the mountains like a hare.

ARGIA [*bewildered*] Gentlemen, there is someone else who can
witness for me. There were two women travellers in this room.
I . . . and another woman.

AMOS [*amiably*] Yes. [*He makes a sign to one of the soldiers, who at once
goes out.*]

ARGIA . . . a peasant-woman.

AMOS [*amiably*] Yes. And where is she now?

ARGIA She ran away. But she can't be far off. That woman . . . can tell you . . . that I'm not what you think. And you will have what you want, just the same. Send out and look for her.

AMOS Up in the mountains?

ARGIA Yes.

AMOS All you can say of your witnesses, is that one is fleeing and the other has fled. [*A pause.*] Madam, we have a surprise for you. [*A pause.*] Your peasant-woman is here. She didn't get very far. Here she is.

[*In a great silence the* QUEEN *appears, escorted by the soldier. The* QUEEN, *pale, and rather stiff, looks round her.* AMOS *points to* ARGIA. *The* QUEEN *comes forward to* ARGIA; *and speaks to her with a slight stammer.*]

THE QUEEN Forgive me, my dear . . . it was all no use . . . I knew they'd have caught me . . . The moment I was so frightened of . . . arrived . . . But I don't think . . . they've caught me in time . . . to hurt me. I managed to fool them . . . you know how . . . I prefer it . . . to be all over at once. Good-bye, my dearest friend. I was so afraid . . . but not so much, now. [*She sways, and sinks slowly to the ground.*]

BIANTE What's the matter?

ARGIA [*kneels down beside the* QUEEN, *and takes her hand. After a while she looks up, and says, as though lost in thought*] She carried poison with her. [*A pause.*] You have killed her.

AMOS [*cutting her short*] You are now completely without accomplices. Say something, why don't you?

BIANTE [*shouting*] You've no one left now!

AMOS It's all over with you, your majesty! Answer us! You are the Queen!

ARGIA [*rises slowly*] Not every eye shall look to the ground. There shall still be someone to stand before you. Yes. I am the Queen! [*A silence.*]

BIANTE She's confessed, Amos. Quick, make your speech for the prosecution.

AMOS [*rises, and thinks for a moment*] If friction is to be stopped, the only way is to remove the cause; if disturbances are to be brought to an end, the only way is to eliminate the disturber. I see only one way to make such eliminations final.

[*The witnesses, perturbed by the decision by which they are to be faced, rise cautiously, first one, then another, trying to efface themselves.*]

AMOS No other method is known whereby revolutions may be at once prudent and rapid; nor any other argument that makes them so persuasive; nor any procedure which more effectively seals dangerous lips and more finally immobilizes enemy hands.

[*The witnesses have cautiously moved towards the door, but at this point* AMOS's *look arrests them.*]

AMOS [*continuing*] Such a method serves also, among other things, to identify the weak pillars; in fact, you will notice that some of our jurymen who have divined the responsibility that is about to face them, are cautiously trying to slip away one by one: they do not realize that, in the course of time, that may render them also liable to furnish proofs of the excellence of the method. It is quite true that the importance of a revolution is in proportion to the number of dead it produces. Biante, it is your duty to pronounce sentence.

BIANTE [*exhausted and swaying, rises, supported by* MAUPA] The revolution has decided that the Queen must die. I order . . . I order . . . [*He cannot go on, he has come to the end:* MAUPA *lifts him back into his chair.*]

AMOS You are no longer in a position to give orders. Your post is vacant. [*He turns to the others.*] The revolution has decided that the Queen must die. The sentence will be carried out during the course of the night.

CURTAIN

Talking

Working in pairs, one of you assumes the role of director; the other takes the character part of *either* Amos or Argia.

Your task is to prepare for the first rehearsal during which you will be required to give a detailed account of how the part is to be played. Make notes on your discussion and include quotations where appropriate.

You will need to consider the following in relation to your chosen character.
■ Changing emotions.
■ Reactions to other characters.
■ What the other characters have to say about you.
■ What your character is thinking and feeling when not speaking.
■ Your movements and stillness.
■ Pause, pace and delivery of lines.

Work sharing

Join with another pair studying the same character. Exchange ideas noting any differences of interpretation. Be prepared to act any part of the script to illustrate the points you have made.

Minor characters in a play, often gems in their own setting, also throw light on events and help us towards a deeper understanding of the behaviour of the major characters.

Talking or writing

Concentrate on some of the characters who have minor parts in this scene.
■ *The Peasants* What advice would you give to actors and actresses preparing for these parts? What clues are there in the text to help you distinguish one peasant from another?
■ *Biante* What do we learn about him and what is his role during this scene?
■ *Raim* Although he says very little during this scene, his presence is crucial. Why? Give as many reasons as possible, *making guesses* about what has happened earlier in the play.

■ *The Queen* The entrance of the Queen marks a climax. How
does the playwright achieve this? How does her death affect
Argia's attitude towards her interrogators?

Drama

Work in groups of at least six and appoint a director for this piece
of work.

Look closely at the final part of this scene from when Argia
says, 'Forgive me. I have been play-acting a little: perhaps too
much.' In consultation with your group:

■ cast the scene. Make use of your previous notes and discussion
about characters;
■ plan and draw the set; decide upon exits and entrances;
■ decide where to place the 'non-speaking' characters;
■ plot the movements for this part of the scene. Include reaction
(non-verbal) to the changing situation;
■ plan the 'shape' of the action. Decide how to deal with Raim's
persistent denials of Argia.

One part you may need to work on is the Queen's entrance
and death. Group improvisation will help to make both the
'dying' and the various reactions to it, more convincing.

2 Finding a focus

The Suspect, Edwin Morgan

In your talk, drama and writing activities, you will have been asked at some time to choose one incident on which to focus your attention. Your teacher may have advised you:
- to keep to the point;
- to cut out irrelevant material;
- to decide where the dramatic climax should come.

All writers have to make decisions about what to include and what to leave out of their work; all directors of plays are concerned with highlighting moments of tension.

The Suspect is an excellent example of a short dramatic poem which focuses our attention on an incident in which a man is being questioned by the police.

Working with this poem and through the ideas it suggests we hope you will gain experience in:
- creating, shaping and improvising short dramatic scenes which show a close attention to detail and a sense of dramatic climax;
- using ideas from your drama as a focus for your writing and, in turn, using your written work to add interest and tension to your drama.

Talk and dramatic activities help us to feel and to understand new experiences and that is why we suggest you begin exploring the ideas in this poem by talking about them in pairs and improvising in groups.

The Suspect

Asked me for a match suddenly/with his hand up
I thought he was after my wallet
gave him a shove/he fell down
dead on the pavement at my feet
he was forty-two, a respectable man they said
anyone can have a bad heart I told the police
but they've held me five hours and don't
tell me the innocent don't feel
guilty in the glaring chair
I didn't kill you/I didn't know you
I did push you/I did fear you
accusing me from the mortuary drawer

like a damned white ghost I don't believe in
– then why were you afraid/are you used to attacks
by men who want a match/what sort
of life you lead/you were bloody quick
with your hands when you pushed him
what did you think he was and do you think
we don't know what you are/take it
all down/the sweat of the innocent by god we'll see
and not by the hundred-watt bulb of the anglepoise either
give him a clip on the ear jack/you
bastard in your shroud if I feared you then
I hate you now you
no I don't you poor dead man I put you there
I don't I don't
but just

if you could get up/to speak for me
I am on trial/do you understand
I am not guilty/whatever the light says
whatever the sweat says
/they've noticed my old scar
to be killed by a dead man is no fight
they're starting again
so/your story is he asked you for a light
– yes suddenly/and put his hand up I thought
he was after my wallet. gave him
a shove. he fell as I told you
dead. it was his heart.
at my feet. as I said

Talking

Working in pairs, first spend time reading and talking about this poem. Re-read 'How To Read a Poem' on page 16 to help you focus your discussion.

You should now be able to answer the following questions.
■ How many characters are referred to in the poem?
■ What do you find significant about the title?
■ Why do you think the poet has chosen to write with the 'voice' of the suspect?
■ How does the suspect's mood change during the course of the poem?
■ Where would you place the dramatic climax in the questioning of the suspect?

Be prepared to give reasons for your answers in your group discussions.

Reading aloud

Prepare *your* interpretation of the poem for sharing with another pair or the whole class.

Your earlier discussion should have helped you to make decisions about:
■ how to allocate speaking parts and how your characters are going to speak;

■ how to use *pause*, *emphasis* and *pace* to heighten tension and
  suggest changes of mood and atmosphere;
■ your positions when you present your reading. Even in a
  classroom it should be possible to find a space which allows
  for limited but effective movement and gesture.
After you have shared your readings, talk about any similarities
and differences in interpretation and presentation.

Drama

During your discussions and readings in pairs, you have been
chiefly concerned with the interrogation of the suspect as seen
from his point of view. In our illustration we have placed this
scene at the centre and chosen some words from the poem as a
title for it.

Your story is he asked you for a light

Improvisation

Working in small groups, take a large sheet of paper and either draw pictures or make notes to suggest *four* other scenes that could be improvised from the situation described in the poem. You could, if you wish, copy the illustration and use the symbol of the anglepoise light to link all five scenes. Choose some appropriate words from the poem as a subtitle for each of your scenes.

You will find plenty of clues in the poem on which to base your speculations about the life of the suspect and the victim both *before* and *after* the alleged crime.

When you have decided upon the content of your scenes, we suggest that each scene is directed by a volunteer from your group.

As a *director* you will have to carry out the following tasks.
- Think about *the form* your improvised scene will take. Some possibilities are mime or mime with dialogue from the poem; your own improvised speech and movement; a 'still-frame'. The use of 'flash-back' as a technique can give you unlimited opportunities for experimenting with time, e.g. a scene in which we learn how the suspect got his scar could take us back to an incident in his childhood.
- Cast your scene. You should include everyone in your group.
- Consider the best use of the space available.
- Decide whether or not to use simple props, costume, sound effects or lighting. *One* or *two* well-chosen items could help sustain concentration and establish characterisation. One subtle way of providing the audience with further information about the victim could be to produce articles found in his pocket, e.g. a letter, a cigarette lighter in perfect working order!
- Discuss and share your ideas with the rest of the group. Don't be afraid to use some of their suggestions.
- Rehearse your group in the order in which the scenes might appear.

When you were younger pupils in the school you probably wanted to spend as little time as possible preparing your work and too much time sharing and showing it. 'Miss, we've finished; can we go first?' is an all too familiar cry in drama lessons.

What you now know is that nothing is ever finished and that often the time spent on preparation is the most valuable and important part of the drama session. It is the time when you are free to experiment with techniques; to be receptive to the ideas of everyone in the group, then to discard some of those ideas in favour of others, knowing why you are doing so.

Your own class will now be very familiar with the ideas in the poem; the real test of whether you have succeeded in focusing down and selecting appropriate images is to invite another class, not familiar with the poem, to be an audience.

Work sharing

In order to present your dramatic sequences as a whole for an audience who has not read the poem, you will now need to discuss the following.

- What adjustments to make in such vital details as the accent, age, occupation of the suspect. Clearing up any discrepancies will help to ensure continuity and credibility when all the scenes are put together.
- What techniques to use to *link* your scenes. Here are some suggestions you might like to try out.
  - Freeze beginnings and endings.
  - The use of lighting – the anglepoise light could be switched on and off.
  - Sound effects or a particular piece of music.
  - The repetition of the interrogation scene using tape-recorded voices to suggest the relentless nature of the questioning.
- The order in which you finally decide to present your scenes. Remember you can repeat parts of scenes for effect.

Writing

- Choose any *one* of the four scenes that you have taken part in and write it as a play script for your teacher to use with another class. At the end, leave a space for constructive comments from those pupils who will either read or act out your script.
  Re-draft your work making use of the feedback you have been given by your fellow pupils.
- Look at several different newspapers for examples and then write the *two* following newspaper articles.
  - Report the death of the victim. Remember you will need to include details in your report which do not appear in the poem, e.g. the name, age, address, occupation of the victim and the suspect.
  - Report the trial of the suspect. You can decide on the verdict.
- Pages from a policeman's notebook. Write what you would expect to find in such a notebook using a new page for notes made:
  - at the scene of the death;
  - during questioning at the police station; and
  - when interviewing witnesses.
- Write a letter which might have been found in the pocket of the victim.
- Spotlight on the suspect: choose one of the people referred to in the poem and take on that person's identity. Write down all you know, think and feel about the suspect from that person's point of view.

STORY

Studies in the Park, Anita Desai

– Turn it off, turn it off! First he listens to the news in Hindi. Directly after, in English. Broom – brroom – brrroom – the voice of doom roars. Next, in Tamil. Then in Punjabi. In Gujarati. What next, my God, what next? Turn it off before I smash it onto his head, fling it out of the window, do nothing of the sort of course, nothing of the sort.

– And my mother. She cuts and fries, cuts and fries. All day I hear her chopping and slicing and the pan of oil hissing. What all does she find to fry and feed us on, for God's sake? Eggplants, potatoes, spinach, shoe soles, newspapers, finally she'll slice me and feed me to my brothers and sisters. Ah, now she's turned on the tap. It's roaring and pouring, pouring and roaring into a bucket without a bottom.

– The bell rings. Voices clash, clatter and break. The tin-and-bottle-man? The neighbours? The police? The Help-the-Blind-man? Thieves and burglars? All of them, all of them, ten or twenty or a hundred of them, marching up the stairs, hammering at the door, breaking in and climbing over me – ten, twenty or a hundred of them.

– Then, worst of all, the milk arrives. In the tallest glass in the house. 'Suno, drink your milk. Good for you, Suno. You need it. Now, before the exams. Must have it, Suno. Drink.' The voice wheedles its way into my ear like a worm. I shudder. The table tips over. The milk runs. The tumbler clangs on the floor. 'Suno, Suno, how will you do your exams?'

– That is precisely what I ask myself. All very well to give me a room – Uncle's been rushed off on a pilgrimage to Hardwar to clear a room for me – and to bring me milk and say, 'Study, Suno, study for your exam.' What about the uproar around me? These people don't know the meaning of the word Quiet. When my mother fills buckets, sloshes the kitchen floor, fries and sizzles things in the pan, she thinks she is being Quiet. The children have never even heard the word, it amazes and puzzles them. On their way back from school they fling their satchels in at my door, then tear in to snatch them back before I tear them to bits. Bawl when I pull their ears, screech when mother whacks them. Stuff themselves with her fries and then smear the grease on my books.

So I raced out of my room, with my fingers in my ears, to scream till the roof fell down about their ears. But the radio suddenly went off, the door to my parents' room suddenly opened and my father appeared, bathed and shaven, stuffed and set up with the news of the world in six different languages – his white *dhoti* blazing, his white shirt crackling, his patent leather pumps glittering. He stopped in the doorway and I stopped on the balls of my feet and wavered. My fingers came out of my ears, my hair came down over my eyes. Then he looked away from me, took his watch out of his pocket and enquired, 'Is the food ready?' in a voice that came out of his nose like the whistle of a punctual train. He skated off towards his meal. I turned and slouched back to my room . . . .

Talking

In pairs, discuss your first impressions, thoughts and feelings after reading Suno's monologue.

Focus your attention on the style Anita Desai has used to

convey both the atmosphere and Suno's mounting frustration with the lack of quiet. Short sentences, several 'non'-sentences, repetition and rhetorical questions are some of the features of this short extract.

Reading

In pairs, prepare to read aloud the first extract as effectively as you can. You will need to consider the following.

■ *Use of accent.* How important is it to use an Indian accent in order to emphasise the speech rhythms and intonation of the speaker?

Some people have a flair for imitating accents whilst others find difficulty in sustaining an authentic voice. Many of our Indian students who speak with a North Kent accent have as much difficulty speaking Suno's thoughts in a convincing manner as anyone else in the class. We suggest that if there is a student or teacher who is able to do this very well, you should listen to his or her interpretation of the passage.

■ *Change of pace and use of pause.* The writer has indicated through her use of punctuation and paragraphing how she intends us to read the story.

■ *Repetition.* How can you use this to make your listeners aware of Suno's feelings about the interminable noise and activity which surround him?

Talking

Working in larger groups, share some of your readings.
Comment on differences in style and presentation.

Writing

■ Using the extract as a model, write your own monologue. Imagine any situation in which an individual under pressure expresses the thoughts in his or her head, e.g.:
 — a student at home or at school trying to study against a background of noise and constant interruptions;
 — a teacher with an unresponsive class;
 — a father with two young children and the week's shopping to do, etc.
■ Re-write Suno's monologue or your own as a poem. We suggest that you:
 — jot down in any order the lines that you intend to keep in your poem;
 — decide on an order which will give your poem an effective form and rhythm;
 — use punctuation thoughtfully in order to make your meaning plain and to indicate how you would like it to be read aloud;
 — think of several titles and choose one which most appropriately expresses the essence of your poem.
 You might wish to redraft your poem several times before you are finally satisfied.

Suno's answer to the pressures upon him was to escape from his family and surroundings. At first he tried to study in the corner teashop and then he discovered the park.
 Over a period of months he came to know the ways of the

park, its rhythms and routine at all times of the day and night.

As the date for the examinations drew nearer, Suno once again experienced a mounting pressure from his family, accompanied by a total inability to function physically and mentally. He felt that he was 'dying' along with all the other students in the park and that, when they entered the examination hall, they would be declared officially dead.

Then I saw the scene that stopped it all, stopped me just before I died.

Hidden behind an oleander was a bench. A woman lay on it, stretched out. She was a Muslim, wrapped in a black *borkha*. I hesitated when I saw this straight, still figure in black on the bench. Just then she lifted a pale, thin hand and lifted her veil. I saw her face. It lay bared, in the black folds of her *borkha*, like a flower, wax-white and composed, like a Persian lily or a tobacco flower at night. She was young. Very young, very pale, beautiful with a beauty I had never come across even in a dream. It caught me and held me tight, tight till I couldn't breathe and couldn't move. She was so white, so still, I saw she was very ill – with anaemia, perhaps, or t.b. Too pale, too white – I could see she was dying. Her head – so still and white it might have been carved if it weren't for this softness, this softness of a flower at night – lay in the lap of a very old man. Very much older than her. With spectacles and a long grey beard like a goat's, or a scholar's. He was looking down at her and caressing her face – so tenderly, so tenderly, I had never seen a hand move so gently and tenderly. Beside them, on the ground, two little girls were playing. Round little girls, rather dirty, drawing lines in the gravel. They stared at me but the man and the woman did not notice me. They never looked at anyone else, only at each other, with an expression that halted me. It was tender, loving, yes, but in an inhuman way, so intense. Divine, I felt, or insane. I stood, half-hidden by the bush, holding my book, and wondered at them. She was ill, I could see, dying. Perhaps she had only a short time to live. Why didn't he take her to the Victoria Zenana Hospital, so close to the park? Who was this man – her husband, her father, a lover? I couldn't make out although I watched them without moving, without breathing. I felt not as if I were staring rudely at strangers, but as if I were gazing at a painting or a sculpture, some work of art. Or seeing a vision. They were still and I stood still and the children stared. Then she lifted her arms above her head and laughed. Very quietly.

I broke away and hurried down the path, in order to leave them alone, in privacy. They weren't a work of art, or a vision, but real, human and alive as no one else in my life had been real and alive. I had only that glimpse of them. But I felt I could never open my books and study or take degrees after that. They belonged to the dead, and now I had seen what being alive meant. The vision burnt the surfaces of my eyes so that they watered as I groped my way up the stairs to the flat. I could hardly find my way to the bed.

It was not just the examination but everything else had suddenly withered and died, gone lifeless and purposeless when compared with this vision. My studies, my family, my life – they all belonged to the dead and only what I had seen in the park had any meaning.

Since I did not know how to span the distance between that beautiful ideal and my stupid, dull existence, I simply lay still and shut my eyes. I kept them shut so as not to see all the puzzled, pleading, indignant faces of my family around me, but I could not shut out their voices.

'Suno, Suno,' I heard them croon and coax and mourn.

'Suno, drink milk.'

'Suno, study.'

'Suno, take the exam.'

And when they tired of being so patient with me and I still would not get up, they began to crackle and spit and storm.

'Get up, Suno.'

'Study, Suno.'

'At once, Suno.'

Only my mother became resigned and gentle. She must have seen something quite out of the ordinary on my face to make her so. I felt her hand on my forehead and heard her say, 'Leave him alone. Let him sleep tonight. He is tired out, that is what it is – he has driven himself too much and now he must sleep.'

Then I heard all of them leave the room. Her hand stayed on my forehead, wet and smelling of onions, and after a bit my tears began to flow from under my lids.

'Poor Suno, sleep,' she murmured.

I went back to the park of course. But now I was changed. I had stopped being a student – I was a 'professional'. My life was dictated by the rules and routine of the park. I still had my book open on the palms of my hands as I strolled but now my eyes strayed without guilt, darting at the young girls walking in pairs, their arms linked, giggling and bumping into each other. Sometimes I stopped to rest on a bench and conversed with one of the old men, told him who my father was and what examination I was preparing for, and allowing him to tell me about his youth, his politics, his philosophy, his youth and again his youth. Or I joked with the other students, sitting on the grass and throwing peanut shells at the chipmunks, and shocking them, I could see, with my irreverence and cynicism about the school, the exam, the system. Once I even nodded at the yoga teacher and exchanged a few words with him. He suggested I join his class and I nodded vaguely and said I would think it over. It might help. My father says I need help. He says I am hopeless but that I need help. I just laugh but I know that he knows I will never appear for the examination, I will never come up to that hurdle or cross it – life has taken a different path for me, in the form of a search, not a race as it is for him, for them.

Yes, it is a search, a kind of perpetual search for me and now that I have accepted it and don't struggle, I find it satisfies me entirely, and I wander about the park as freely as a prince in his palace garden. I look over the benches, I glance behind the bushes, and wonder if I shall ever get another glimpse of that strange vision that set me free. I never have but I keep hoping, wishing.

Reading

Read the ending of the short story.

Talking

- Do you find Suno's transformation surprising or difficult to accept?
- Mention some phrases which indicate the profound effect that the 'scene' had on him.
- Do you admire Suno's rejection of his family's expectations?
- Do you consider his attitude towards his family to be selfish and uncaring?
- How does the writer use the scene of the dying woman as a focus for:
  - Suno's personal development;
  - the overall shape of her story?

A key quotation from this part of the story makes a very important comment about how Suno records his memory of the scene. He sees it in visual form as if he were 'gazing at a painting or a sculpture, some work of art'.

Had Suno been an artist, it is likely that he would have translated his memory into some art form. Art students are often asked to work from a piece of descriptive prose or poetry. Some of you might choose to focus on the description of the scene in the park as a basis for your work in art.

Quite often, however, it is the painting or sculpture which provides the stimulus for a story or poem. One of our most distinguished poets, R. S. Thomas, was so inspired by some of the Impressionist paintings in the Louvre, that he used thirty-three of them as starting points for poems included in his collection, *Between Here and Now*. 'Family Reunion' is the title of a painting by Bazille and a poem by R. S. Thomas.

Study the picture and poem in detail and share your thoughts and feelings (not your likes and dislikes!) about the statements being made by both the artist and the poet.

Family Reunion

In groups
    under the tree,
none of them sorry
for having partaken
      of its knowledge.

Sex? They wanted
    it. Children?
Why not?
    And clothes, clothes:
how they outdo
      their background.

Their looks challenge
    us to find
      where they failed.

Well-dressed, well-
fed; their servants
    are out of sight,
snatching a moment
      to beget offspring
who are to overturn all this.

Family Reunion

Tea Garden

Writing

Look closely at the painting 'Tea Garden' by Eric Holt.

Jot down any ideas which come to mind as you look at *all* or *part* of the picture. Do not attempt to describe the painting; try to capture the mood and atmosphere through a personal response.

Select your material and choose your words and images. Write your first draft in prose form. Re-draft, organising your writing into appropriate lines of verse, punctuating it so that your thoughts and feelings are made quite clear to your reader. Read aloud.

VERSE

Note to the Hurrying Man, Brian Patten

All day I sit here doing nothing but
watching how at daybreak
birds fly out and return no fatter
when it's over. Yet hurrying about this room
you would have me do something similar;
would have me make myself a place
in that sad traffic you call a world.
　　Don't hurry me into it; offer
no excuses, no apologies.
Until their brains snap open
I have no love for those who rush
about its mad business;
put their children on a starting line and push
into Christ knows what madness.

　　You will not listen.
'Work at life!' you scream,
and working I see you rushing everywhere,
so fast most times you ignore
two quarters of your half a world.
　　If all slow things are useless
and take no active part in nor justify your ignorance
that's fine; but why bother screaming after me?
Afraid perhaps to come to where I've stopped
in case you find
into some slow and glowing countryside
　　yourself escaping.
Screams measure and keep up the distance between us:
　　Be quieter –
I really do need to escape;
take the route you might take
if ever this hurrying is over.

Talking

Working in pairs or small groups, discuss the similarities and differences in theme, treatment, style and form between this poem and the prose extract from *Studies in the Park.* Make notes on your discussion.

　　To help you to deepen your own understanding of form, at some point focus your attention on Brian Patten's use of:

■ two verses;
■ two long sentences and one short one in the first verse;
■ three semi-colons in the first verse;
■ one short sentence to begin verse two;
■ use of direct speech;
■ four long sentences and two shorter ones in the second verse;
■ one rhetorical question.

Reading aloud   Working in a small group, choose either your prose or poetry monologue to share with the others.

Decide how to use some or all of the poem *Note to the Hurrying Man* as a group answer to the pressures you have all written about and expressed in your writing.

You could decide to separate each of your readings by using lines from Patten's poem as a chorus or to use the whole poem at the end of your group's reading.

Drama   Prepare appropriate sound effects and linking music to accompany the creative writing of the people in your group.

You might decide to present your work under the general title of 'Pressures' and to develop your ideas by adding other examples from poems, plays, and short stories in which an individual voice expresses a feeling of pressure from family, work, society or within himself or herself. You will find some examples in this book.

Aim at variety in mood, style and pace in both your choice of material and the order in which you present it.

Rehearse your final script and prepare for presentation to another class as a stimulus for their thinking, talk and creative writing.

3 Shifting viewpoints

Optical illusions

What do you see?   (now . . . look again!)

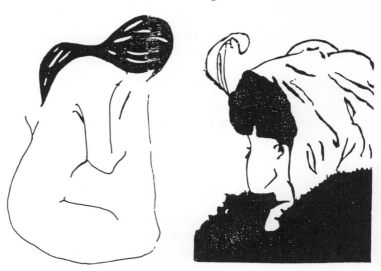

VERSE

The Centre of Attention, Daniel Hoffman

This is a poem in which the poet, as one spectator in a crowd, witnesses a dramatic event. An adult male has climbed to the top of a pylon; a crowd of onlookers and disaster crews gather; the man threatens to jump.

The Centre of Attention

As grit swirls in the wind the word spreads.
On pavement approaching the bridge a crowd
Springs up like mushrooms.
They are hushed at first, intently

Looking. At the top of the pylon
The target of their gaze leans toward them.
The sky sobs
With the sirens of disaster crews

Careening toward the crowd with nets,
Ladders, resuscitation gear, their First
Aid attendants antiseptic in white duck.
The police, strapped into their holsters,

Exert themselves in crowd-control. They can't
Control the situation.
Atop the pylon there's a man who threatens
Violence. He shouts, *I'm gonna jump* –

And from the river of upturned faces
– Construction workers pausing in their construction work,
Shoppers diverted from their shopping,
The idlers relishing this diversion

In the vacuity of their day – arises
A chorus of cries – *Jump!*
Jump! and *No—*
Come down! Come down! Maybe, if he can hear them,

They seem to be saying *Jump down!* The truth is,
The crowd cannot make up its mind.
This is a tough decision. The man beside me
Reaches into his lunchbox and lets him have it,

Jump! before he bites his sandwich,
While next to him a young blonde clutches
Her handbag to her breasts and moans
Don't Don't Don't so very softly

You'd think she was afraid of being heard.
The will of the people is divided.
Up there he hasn't made his mind up either.
He has climbed and climbed on spikes imbedded in the pylon

To get where he has arrived at.
Is he sure now that this is where he was going?
He looks down one way into the river.
He looks down the other way into the people.

He seems to be looking for something
Or for somebody in particular.
Is there anyone here who is that person
Or can give him what it is that he needs?

From the back of a firetruck a ladder teeters.
Inching along, up, up up up up, a policeman
Holds on with one hand, sliding it on ahead of him.
In the other, outstretched, a pack of cigarettes.

Soon the man will decide between
The creature comfort of one more smoke
And surcease from being a creature.
Meanwhile the crowd calls *Jump!* and calls *Come down!*

Now, his cassock billowing in the bulges of Death's black flag,
A priest creeps up the ladder too.
What will the priest and the policeman together
Persuade the man to do?

He has turned his back to them.
He has turned away from everyone.
His solitariness is nearly complete.
He is alone with his decision.

No one on the ground or halfway into the sky can know
The hugeness of the emptiness that surrounds him.
All of his senses are orphans.
His ribs are cold andirons.

Does he regret his rejection of furtive pills,
Of closet noose or engine idling in closed garage?
A body will plummet through shrieking air,
The audience dumb with horror, the spattered street . . .

The world he has left is as small as toys at his feet.
Where he stands, though nearer the sun, the wind is chill.
He clutches his arms – a caress, or is he trying
Merely to warm himself with his arms?

The people below, their necks are beginning to ache.
They are getting impatient for this diversion
To come to some conclusion. The priest
Inches further narrowly up the ladder.

The centre of everybody's attention
For some reason has lit up a butt. He sits down.
He looks down on the people gathered, and sprinkles
Some of his ashes upon them.

Before he is halfway down
The crowd is half-dispersed.
It was his aloneness that clutched them together.
They were spellbound by his despair

And now each rung brings him nearer,
Nearer to their condition
Which is not sufficiently interesting
To detain them from business or idleness either,

Or is too close to a despair
They do not dare
Exhibit before a crowd
Or admit to themselves they share.

Now the police are taking notes
On clipboards, filling the forms.
He looks round as though searching for what he came down for.
Traffic flows over the bridge.

Talking and drama

Working in groups, read the poem aloud or quietly to
yourselves. You must pay attention to the punctuation in order to
understand the poem.
   Use the ideas in the poem as a basis for an improvisation. We
suggest *one* way of starting might be to appoint a director for
your group who will lead the discussion and direct the action,
and then to work on some of the following ideas.

■ Focus on 'the crowd'. Talk about the following.
   – Who are the individuals who make up the crowd –
      construction workers, shoppers, idlers, etc?
   – What is each doing before the 'word spreads'?
   – What is each person feeling, doing as s/he stands hushed at
      the bottom of the pylon?
   – How does each person react to (a) the 'target of their gaze'
      leaning 'toward them'? and (b) 'the sirens of' the 'disaster
      crews'?
■ Give yourselves an identity and a role.
   – Improvise the beginning of the scene where the crowd
      gathers and responds to the situation. Use appropriate
      dialogue to accompany your actions and to communicate

your feelings.
– Freeze the action and come together as a group.
■ Talk about the following – in role.
– The ways in which the crowd behaves during the rest of the poem.
– How might you, as an individual, respond to the policeman's handing a packet of cigarettes to the man and the priest's attempts to persuade him to abandon his position?
– We are told that:

> 'their necks are beginning to ache.
> They are getting impatient for this diversion
> To come to some conclusion.'

At what point do *you* decide you are no longer interested and drift away?
■ Focus on the poet as spectator in the role of a narrator and be guided by his voice as he leads you through the action.
■ Focus on 'the centre of attention'. Give him a background and a reason for being in this position. Improvise the events which might have led up to the incident described in the poem.
■ Tell another person about the incident in which you were caught up. As the 'listener' asks questions to find out more about what happened, the answers could come in the form of a series of 'flash-backs'.

You will probably think of other ways of presenting this human dilemma, in practical terms, which do not treat the subject matter in a light, superficial manner.
Which ever way you choose, the director should make sure that everyone in the group is included.

Making a film

An exciting way of presenting the ideas in this poem is to view them through the eyes of a camera. Some of you will have used a video camera and will have scripted and shot your own films. For those of you not so familiar with this art form, we include:
■ a few technical terms;
■ the beginning and the ending of the poem as it might appear as a television script – the production sheet;
■ a storyboard;
■ a series of diagrams explaining camera shots.

Technical terms

b/g background
C.U. Close-Up
f/g foreground
F/X Sound Effects
High Angle (H/A) This angle allows the viewer an opportunity to observe the whole situation at a glance. It often implies remoteness

Low Angle (L/A)   The low angle lowers the viewpoint thereby emphasising the imposing character of a person or object

L.S.   Long Shot

M.C.U.   Medium Close-Up

M.L.S.   Medium Long Shot

M.S.   Medium Shot

Over Shoulder (O/S)   As the name implies it is a shot from behind a character and often includes the shoulder of the person in the corner of the shot

Pan   A horizontal movement of the camera about a fixed axis. The pan changes the centre of attention and demonstrates spatial relationships

Point of View (P.O.V.)   The P.O.V. shot provides a 'viewer's eye view'. It assumes that the viewer is a part of the plot and serves to draw him further into the action

Tilt   A vertical movement of the camera about a fixed axis. In a similar way to the pan it demonstrates spatial relationships. It also emphasises height or depth

Track   The physical movement of the camera and its mount horizontally. Tracking gives the attitude of inspection

X.L.S. or *W/S*   Extra Long Shot or Wide Shot

Zoom   A quick, or slow, change from a long shot to a close-up made possible by the zoom lens. The zoom concentrates our attention on a particular point, providing an emphasis to the scene

Production sheet

SHOT No	LENS			F/X
1	M.S.	L/A track along pavement to reveal feet	AS GRIT SWIRLS IN THE WIND THE WORD SPREADS. (More feet join)	Wind
		Tilt up to faces — slow zoom in to C.U.	ON THE PAVEMENT APPROACHING THE BRIDGE A CROWD	Crowd murmur
			SPRINGS UP LIKE MUSHROOMS.	Distant sirens
2	C.U.		(Another face looking upwards) THEY ARE HUSHED AT FIRST, INTENTLY LOOKING. AT THE TOP OF THE PYLON	

SHOT No	LENS			F/X
3	X.L.S.	Crowd f/g. Man on bridge b/g. Slow zoom in to M.L.S.	THE TARGET OF THEIR GAZE LEANS TOWARD THEM.	Sirens increasing
			(Man momentarily overbalances)	Crowd gasp
			THE SKY SOBS WITH THE SIRENS OF DISASTER CREWS	
4	C.U.	Feet running past camera		Running Shouting
5	C.U.		(Fireman rolls up door, rear of fire engine)	Door opens
			CAREENING TOWARD THE CROWD WITH NETS, LADDERS, ⟋ RESUSCITATION	
6	C.U.		GEAR, THEIR FIRST.	
			(Hands opening case – unpacking gear)	
7	C.U.		(Man watches the commotion below him)	General atmosphere continues
			AID ATTENDANTS ANTISEPTIC IN WHITE DUCK.	
8	C.U.		(Policeman talking to his radio)	Radio chatter
			THE POLICE, STRAPPED INTO THEIR HOLSTERS,	
9	C.U.		(Feet running past camera)	
10	C.U.		(Firemen unloading a ladder)	Clatter
			EXERT THEMSELVES IN CROWD-CONTROL. THEY CAN'T ⟋	
11	C.U.		(Hand picks up megaphone from car seat)	
			CONTROL THE SITUATION.	
			(Door slams shut)	Car door

SHOT No	LENS			F/X
12	C.U.		(Journalist's notebook. We see copious notes)	
13	L.S.	P.O.V. shot running towards crowd Camera enters the gathering — people in front part to allow camera through	ATOP THE PYLON THERE'S A MAN WHO THREATENS	Crowd murmur
	P.O.V.	We emerge from the crowd	(Police officer stands in clearing. As the camera emerges from front of crowd he turns — looks over his shoulder — then looks back)	
			VIOLENCE. / HE SHOUTS, *I'M GONNA JUMP* —	Echo 'Jump'
		Camera follows policeman's gaze. Tilt up — zoom in to M.S.		
14	L.S.	H/A	(Upturned faced) AND FROM THE RIVER OF UPTURNED FACES	'Jump'
15	M.L.S.		(Construction worker turns to camera) — CONSTRUCTION WORKERS PAUSING IN THEIR CONSTRUCTION WORK,	'Jump'
16	M.L.S.		(Lady with shopping stops — looks up) SHOPPERS DIVERTED FROM THEIR SHOPPING, THE IDLERS RELISHING / THIS DIVERSION	'Jump'
17	M.L.S.		(Man caught in traffic sits back in driver's seat and watches the man on pylon)	'Jump'

SHOT No	LENS			F/X
18	L.S.	O/S H/A Back of man f/g. Crowd b/g	IN THE VACUITY OF THEIR DAY — ARISES	

Last 3 verses

SHOT No	LENS			F/X
51	M.C.U.	Pan down with man	(Man climbs down ladder) AND NOW EACH RUNG BRINGS HIM NEARER,	
		Slow zoom out to M.L.S. to reveal dispersing crowd	———————————— NEARER TO THEIR CONDITION (Crowd dividing — leaving in various directions) WHICH IS NOT SUFFICIENTLY INTERESTING	Crowd atmosphere lessening
52	M.C.U.		(Man in car still watching figure on bridge) TO DETAIN THEM FROM BUSINESS OR IDLENESS EITHER,	
		Allow man to drive out of frame	(Car beeps behind, driver hurriedly starts up and moves on)	Car horn
53	M.C.U.		(Construction worker turns back to his work) OR IS TOO CLOSE TO A DESPAIR THEY DO NOT DARE	
54	M.C.U.		EXHIBIT BEFORE A CROWD	
		Pan with lady & hold as she walks away	(Lady with shopping trolley walks on) OR ADMIT TO THEMSELVES THEY SHARE.	

SHOT No	LENS			F/X
55	C.U.	Pan up to face	(Journalist's notebook)	
			Journalist narrates next two lines	
			NOW THE POLICE ARE TAKING NOTES ON CLIPBOARDS, FILLING THE FORMS.	
56	C.U.	Follow man down	(Man descends ladder — cigarette in mouth)	
			HE LOOKS ROUND	
		Follow cigarette butt as it falls to the ground	(Man pauses, looks down, takes cigarette and drops it)	
			AS THOUGH SEARCHING FOR WHAT HE CAME DOWN FOR.	Traffic noise
			(Cigarette lands on road below)	
			TRAFFIC FLOWS OVER THE BRIDGE.	
			(Cigarette is run over by car tyre)	
		Tilt up and zoom out L.S.		Fade out

Storyboard

On the storyboard, a drawing is made to represent each shot. The drawings of the first two shots are shown here as an example.

AS GRIT SWIRLS IN THE WIND
THE WORD SPREADS.
ON THE PAVEMENT —
. . . . —LIKE MUSHROOMS.

SHOT Nº 1

THEY ARE HUSHED AT FIRST
– . . .
AT THE TOP OF THE PYLON

SHOT Nº. 2

55

Different types of camera shot

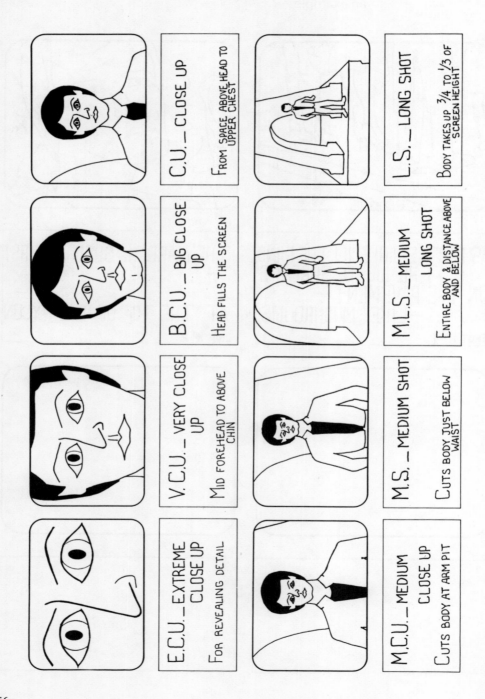

C.U. – CLOSE UP
From space above head to upper chest

L.S. – LONG SHOT
Body takes up 3/4 to 1/3 of screen height

B.C.U. – BIG CLOSE UP
Head fills the screen

M.L.S. – MEDIUM LONG SHOT
Entire body & distance above and below

V.C.U. – VERY CLOSE UP
Mid forehead to above chin

M.S. – MEDIUM SHOT
Cuts body just below waist

E.C.U. – EXTREME CLOSE UP
For revealing detail

M.C.U. – MEDIUM CLOSE UP
Cuts body at arm pit

Talking, writing and drawing

Working in groups, study all the material. Talk about and share your own experiences of photography.

■ Write a film script for all or any part of the poem not yet scripted.

■ Draw the storyboard which might have been prepared for the first six verses of the poem. Use the example we have provided to get you started.

Writing

■ Write your own story, entitled 'The Centre of Attention', about the events which led up to the incident described in the poem.

■ As an onlooker, a member of the crowd, describe what happened and how you felt at the conclusion of the incident. Start with the words of the last verse as a beginning to your account of what happened.

> Now the police are taking notes
> On clipboards, filling the forms

Many poets are inspired to write as a result of having read news items.

■ Write the newspaper article which might have occasioned this poem.

■ Write your own poem based on any recent news item which has moved you to anger, laughter or tears.

NOVEL

To Kill a Mockingbird, Harper Lee

All the action in this story takes place in a small community in the south of the United States during the early 1930s.

The novel begins when Scout Finch, the narrator, is nearly six years old and it ends three years later.

During this period she and her elder brother, Jem, are involved in many learning experiences which deeply affect their attitudes towards their lawyer father, Atticus, and their neighbours. The major incident in the story is the trial of Tom Robinson, a black man, accused of the rape of a white girl.

One of the interesting aspects of the novel is that the reader experiences this and other dramatic events through the changing viewpoints of the young storyteller.

Early on in the novel, her father tries to explain to Scout the importance of seeing things from the other person's point of view. 'First of all,' he said, 'if you can learn a simple trick, Scout, you'll get along a lot better with all kinds of folks. You never really understand a person until you consider things from his point of view – until you climb into his skin and walk around in it.'

One of the characters whose skin the children are forced to 'walk around in' is the much feared and hated Mrs Henry Lafayette Dubose, 'the meanest old woman who ever lived'.

Mrs Dubose lived alone except for a Negro girl in constant attendance, two doors up the street from us in a house with steep front steps and a dog-trot hall. She was very old; she spent most of each day in bed and the rest of it in a wheel-chair. It was rumoured that she kept a C.S.A. pistol concealed among her numerous shawls and wraps.

Jem and I hated her. If she was on the porch when we passed, we would be raked by her wrathful gaze, subjected to ruthless interrogation regarding our behaviour, and given a melancholy prediction on what we would amount to when we grew up, which was always nothing. We had long ago given up the idea of walking past her house on the opposite side of the street; that only made her raise her voice and let the whole neighbourhood in on it.

We could do nothing to please her. If I said as sunnily as I could, 'Hey, Mrs Dubose,' I would receive for an answer, 'Don't you say hey to me, you ugly girl! You say good afternoon, Mrs Dubose!'

She was vicious. Once she heard Jem refer to our father as 'Atticus' and her reaction was apoplectic. Besides being the sassiest, most disrespectful mutts whoever passed her way, we were told that it was quite a pity our father had not remarried after our mother's death. A lovelier lady than our mother never lived, she said, and it was heart-breaking the way Atticus Finch let her children run wild. I did not remember our mother, but Jem did – he would tell me about her sometimes – and he went livid when Mrs Dubose shot us this message.

Jem, having survived Boo Radley, a mad dog and other terrors, had concluded that it was cowardly to stop at Miss Rachel's front steps and wait, and had decreed that we must run as far as the post office corner each evening to meet Atticus coming from work. Countless evenings Atticus would find Jem furious at something Mrs Dubose had said when we went by.

'Easy does it, son,' Atticus would say. 'She's an old lady and she's ill. You just hold your head high and be a gentleman. Whatever she says to you, it's your job not to let her make you mad.'

Jem would say she must not be very sick, she hollered so. When the three of us came to her house, Atticus would sweep off his hat, wave gallantly to her and say, 'Good evening, Mrs Dubose! You look like a picture this evening.'

I never heard Atticus say like a picture of what. He would tell her the courthouse news, and would say he hoped with all his heart she'd have a good day tomorrow. He would return his hat to his head, swing me to his shoulders in her very presence, and we would go home in the twilight. It was times like these when I thought my father, who hated guns and had never been to any wars, was the bravest man who ever lived.

The day after Jem's twelfth birthday his money was burning up his pockets, so we headed for town in the early afternoon. Jem thought he had enough to buy a miniature steam-engine for himself and a twirling baton for me.

*

Mrs Dubose was stationed on her porch when we went by.

'Where are you two going at this time of day?' she shouted. 'Playing hooky, I suppose. I'll just call up the principal and tell him!' She put her hands on the wheels of her chair and executed a perfect right face.

'Aw, it's Saturday, Mrs Dubose,' said Jem.

'Makes no difference if it's Saturday,' she said obscurely. 'I wonder if your father knows where you are?'

'Mrs Dubose, we've been goin' to town by ourselves since we were this high.' Jem placed his hand palm down about two feet above the sidewalk.

'Don't you lie to me!' she yelled. 'Jeremy Finch, Maudie Atkinson told me you broke down her scuppernong arbor this morning. She's going to tell your father and then you'll wish you never saw the light of day! If you aren't sent to the reform school before next week, my name's not Dubose!'

Jem, who hadn't been near Miss Maudie's scuppernong arbor since last summer, and who knew Miss Maudie wouldn't tell Atticus if he had, issued a general denial.

'Don't you contradict me!' Mrs Dubose bawled. 'And *you* –' she pointed an arthritic finger at me '– what are you doing in those overalls? You should be in a dress and camisole, young lady! You'll grow up waiting on tables if somebody doesn't change your ways – a Finch waiting on tables at the O.K. Café – hah!'

I was terrified. The O.K. Café was a dim organisation on the north side of the square. I grabbed Jem's hand but he shook me loose.

'Come on, Scout,' he whispered. 'Don't pay any attention to her, just hold your head high and be a gentleman.'

But Mrs Dubose held us: 'Not only a Finch waiting on tables but one in the courthouse lawing for niggers!'

Jem stiffened. Mrs Dubose's shot had gone home and she knew it:

'Yes indeed, what has this world come to when a Finch goes against his raising? I'll tell you!' She put her hand to her mouth. When she drew it away, it trailed a long silver thread of saliva. 'Your father's no better than the niggers and trash he works for!'

Jem was scarlet. I pulled at his sleeve, and we were followed up the sidewalk by a philippic on our family's moral degeneration, the major premise of which was that half the Finches were in the asylum anyway, but if our mother were living we would not have come to such a state.

I wasn't sure what Jem resented most, but I took umbrage at Mrs Dubose's assessment of the family's mental hygiene. I had become almost accustomed to hearing insults aimed at Atticus. But this was the first one coming from an adult. Except for her remarks about Atticus, Mrs Dubose's attack was only routine. There was a hint of summer in the air – in the shadows it was cool, but the sun was warm, which meant good times coming: no school and Dill.

Jem bought his steam-engine and we went by Elmore's for my baton. Jem took no pleasure in his acquisition; he jammed it in his pocket and walked silently beside me towards home. On the way home I nearly hit Mr Link Deas, who said, 'Look out now, Scout!' when I missed a toss, and when we approached Mrs Dubose's house my baton was grimy from having picked it up out of the dirt so many times.

She was not on the porch.

In later years, I sometimes wondered exactly what made Jem do it, what made him break the bonds of 'You just be a gentleman, son,' and the phase of self-conscious rectitude he had recently entered. Jem had probably stood as much guff about Atticus lawing for niggers as I had, and I took it for granted that he kept his temper – he had a naturally tranquil disposition and a slow fuse. At the time, however, I thought the only explanation for what he did was that for a few minutes he simply went mad.

What Jem did was something I'd do as a matter of course had I not been under Atticus's interdict, which I assumed included not fighting horrible old ladies. We had just come to her gate when Jem snatched my baton and ran flailing wildly up the steps into Mrs Dubose's front yard, forgetting everything Atticus had said, forgetting that she packed a pistol under her shawls, forgetting that if Mrs Dubose missed, her girl Jessie probably wouldn't.

He did not begin to calm down until he had cut the tops off every camellia bush Mrs Dubose owned, until the ground was littered with green buds and leaves. He bent my baton against his knee, snapped it in two and threw it down.

By that time I was shrieking. Jem yanked my hair, said he didn't care, he'd do it again if he got a chance, and if I didn't shut up he'd pull every hair out of my head. I didn't shut up and he kicked me. I lost my balance and fell on my face. Jem picked me up roughly but looked like he was sorry. There was nothing to say.

We did not choose to meet Atticus coming home that evening. We skulked around the kitchen until Calpurnia threw us out. By some voo-doo system Calpurnia seemed to know all about it. She was a less than satisfactory source of palliation, but she did give Jem a hot biscuit-and-butter which he tore in half and shared with me. It tasted like cotton.

We went to the living-room. I picked up a football magazine, found a picture of Dixie Howell, showed it to Jem and said, 'This looks like you.' That was the nicest thing I could think to say to him, but it was no help. He sat by the windows, hunched down in a rocking-chair, scowling, waiting. Daylight faded.

Two geological ages later, we heard the soles of Atticus's shoes scrape the front steps. The screen door slammed, there was a pause – Atticus was at the hat-rack in the hall – and we heard him call, 'Jem!' His voice was like the winter wind.

Atticus switched on the ceiling-light in the living-room and found us there, frozen still. He carried my baton in one hand; its filthy yellow tassel trailed on the rug. He held out his other hand; it contained fat camellia buds.

'Jem,' he said, 'are you responsible for this?'

'Yes sir.'

'Why'd you do it?'

Jem said softly, 'She said you lawed for niggers and trash.'

'You did this because she said that?'

Jem's lips moved, but his, 'Yes sir,' was inaudible.

'Son, I have no doubt that you've been annoyed by your contemporaries about me lawing for niggers, as you say, but to do something like this to a sick old lady is inexcusable. I strongly advise you to go down and have a talk with Mrs Dubose,' said Atticus. 'Come straight home afterwards.'

Jem did not move.

'Go on,' I said.

I followed Jem out of the living-room. 'Come back here,' Atticus said to me. I came back.

Atticus picked up the *Mobile Press* and sat down in the rocking-chair Jem had vacated. For the life of me, I did not understand how he could sit there in cold blood and read a newspaper when his only son stood an excellent chance of being murdered with a Confederate Army relic. Of course Jem antagonised me sometimes until I could kill him, but when it came down to it he was all I had. Atticus did not seem to realise this, or if he did he didn't care.

I hated him for that, but when you are in trouble you become easily tired; soon I was hiding in his lap and his arms were around me.

'You're mighty big to be rocked,' he said.

'You don't care what happens to him,' I said. 'You just send him on to get shot at when all he was doin' was standin' up for you.'

Atticus pushed my head under his chin. 'It's not time to worry yet,' he said. 'I never thought Jem'd be the one to lose his head over this – thought I'd have more trouble with you.'

I said I didn't see why we had to keep our heads anyway, that nobody I knew at school had to keep his head about anything.

'Scout,' said Atticus, 'when summer comes you'll have to keep your head about far worse things ... it's not fair for you and Jem, I know that, but sometimes we have to make the best of things, and the way we conduct ourselves when the chips are down – well, all I can say is, when you and Jem are grown, maybe you'll look back on this with some compassion and some feeling that I didn't let you down. This case, Tom Robinson's case, is something that goes to the essence of a man's conscience – Scout, I couldn't go to church and worship God if I didn't try to help that man.'

'Atticus, you must be wrong. . . .'

'How's that?'

'Well, most folks seem to think they're right and you're wrong. . . .'

'They're certainly entitled to think that, and they're entitled to full respect for their opinions,' said Atticus, 'but before I can live with other folks I've got to live with myself. The one thing that doesn't abide by majority rule is a person's conscience.'

When Jem returned, he found me still in Atticus's lap. 'Well, son?' said Atticus. He set me on my feet, and I made a secret reconnaissance of Jem. He seemed to be all in one piece, but he had a queer look on his face. Perhaps she had given him a dose of calomel.

'I cleaned it up for her and said I was sorry, but I ain't, and that I'd work on 'em every Saturday and try to make 'em grow back out.'

'There was no point in saying you were sorry if you aren't,' said Atticus. 'Jem, she's old and ill. You can't hold her responsible for what she says and does. Of course, I'd rather she'd have said it to me than to either of you, but we can't always have our 'druthers.'

Jem seemed fascinated by a rose in the carpet. 'Atticus,' he said, 'she wants me to read to her.'

'Read to her?'

'Yes sir. She wants me to come every afternoon after school and Saturdays and read to her out loud for two hours. Atticus, do I have to?'

'Certainly.'

'But she wants me to do it for a month.'

'Then you'll do it for a month.'

Jem planted his big toe delicately in the centre of the rose and pressed it in. Finally he said, 'Atticus, it's all right on the side-walk but inside it's – it's all dark and creepy. There's shadows and things on the ceiling. . . .'

*

The following week found us back at Mrs Dubose's. The alarm clock had ceased sounding, but Mrs Dubose would release us with, 'That'll do,' so late in the afternoon Atticus would be home reading the paper when we returned. Although her fits had passed off, she was in every other way her old self; when Sir Walter Scott became involved in lengthy descriptions of moats and castles, Mrs Dubose would become bored and pick on us:

'Jeremy Finch, I told you you'd live to regret tearing up my camellias. You regret it now, don't you?'

Jem would say he certainly did.

'Thought you could kill my Snow-on-the-Mountain, did you? Well, Jessie says the top's growing back out. Next time you'll know how to do it right, won't you? You'll pull it up by the roots, won't you?'

Jem would say he certainly would.

'Don't you mutter at me, boy! You hold up your head and say yes ma'am. Don't guess you feel like holding it up, though, with your father what he is.'

Jem's chin would come up, and he would gaze at Mrs Dubose with a face devoid of resentment. Through the weeks he had cultivated an expression of polite and detached interest, which he would present to her in answer to her most blood-curdling inventions.

At last the day came. When Mrs Dubose said, 'That'll do,' one afternoon, she added. 'And that's all. Good-day to you.'

It was over. We bounded down the sidewalk on a spree of sheer relief, leaping and howling.

That spring was a good one: the days grew longer and gave us more playing time. Jem's mind was occupied mostly with the vital statistics of every college football player in the nation. Every night Atticus would read us the sports pages of the newspapers. Alabama might go to the Rose Bowl again this year, judging from its prospects, not one of whose names we could pronounce. Atticus was in the middle of Windy Seaton's column one evening when the telephone rang.

He answered it, then went to the hat-rack in the hall. 'I'm going down to Mrs Dubose's for a while,' he said. 'I won't be long.'

But Atticus stayed away until long past my bedtime. When he returned he was carrying a candy box. Atticus sat down in the living-room and put the box on the floor beside his chair.

'What'd she want?' asked Jem.

We had not seen Mrs Dubose for over a month. She was never on the porch any more when we passed.

'She's dead, son,' said Atticus. 'She died a few minutes ago.'

'Oh,' said Jem. 'Well.'

'Well is right,' said Atticus. 'She's not suffering any more. She was sick for a long time. Son, didn't you know what her fits were?'

Jem shook his head.

'Mrs Dubose was a morphine addict,' said Atticus. 'She took it as a pain-killer for years. The doctor put her on it. She'd have spent the rest of her life on it and died without so much agony, but she was too contrary –'

'Sir?' said Jem.

Atticus said, 'Just before your escapade she called me to make her will. Dr Reynolds told her she had only a few months left. Her business affairs were in perfect order but she said, "There's still one thing out of order."'

'What was that?' Jem was perplexed.

'She said she was going to leave this world beholden to nothing and nobody. Jem, when you're sick as she was, it's all right to take anything to make it easier, but it wasn't all right for her. She said she meant to break herself of it before she died, and that's what she did.'

Jem said, 'You mean that's what her fits were?'

'Yes, that's what they were. Most of the time you were reading to her I doubt if she heard a word you said. Her whole mind and body were concentrated on that alarm clock. If you hadn't fallen into her hands, I'd have made you go read to her anyway. It may have been some distraction. There was another reason –'

'Did she die free?' asked Jem.

'As the mountain air,' said Atticus. 'She was conscious to the last, almost. Conscious,' he smiled, 'and cantankerous. She still disapproved heartily of my doings, and said I'd probably spend the rest of my life bailing you out of jail. She had Jessie fix you this box –'

Atticus reached down and picked up the candy-box. He

handed it to Jem.

Jem opened the box. Inside, surrounded by wads of damp cotton, was a white, waxy, perfect camellia. It was a Snow-on-the-Mountain.

Jem's eyes nearly popped out of his head. 'Old hell-devil, old hell-devil!' he screamed, flinging it down. 'Why can't she leave me alone?'

In a flash Atticus was up and standing over him. Jem buried his face in Atticus's shirt front. 'Sh-h,' he said. 'I think that was her way of telling you – everything's all right now, Jem, everything's all right. You know, she was a great lady.'

'A lady?' Jem raised his head. His face was scarlet. 'After all those things she said about you, a lady?'

'She was. She had her own views about things, a lot different from mine, maybe . . . son, I told you that if you hadn't lost your head I'd have made you go read to her. I wanted you to see something about her – I wanted you to see what real courage is, instead of getting the idea that courage is a man with a gun in his hand. It's when you know you're licked before you begin but you begin anyway and you see it through no matter what. You rarely win, but sometimes you do. Mrs Dubose won, all ninety-eight pounds of her. According to her views, she died beholden to nothing and nobody. She was the bravest person I ever knew.'

Jem picked up the candy-box and threw it in the fire. He picked up the camellia, and when I went off to bed I saw him fingering the wide petals. Atticus was reading the paper.

Talking

- Is the reader's impression of Mrs Dubose influenced by the fact that she is seen through the eyes of a child?
- How does this account gain from being written in the first person narrative?
- What advantages would there be in using a 'third person' viewpoint?
- What does the reader learn about Atticus as a father and as a member of the community during this part of the story?
- Is there any indication that the children have learned anything from their experience?

Writing

- Re-tell the incident from Atticus' point of view. You might choose to write in diary form or a letter to his brother or sister in which, as part of other news, he mentions Jem's destruction of the camellias and how he dealt with the situation.
- Write a short dialogue between Jem and Scout in which they discuss the death of Mrs Dubose.
- Set another scene ten years in the future. Scout and Jem are remembering the incident of the camellias and other events fixed in their memories during that three years.

  If you have read the whole book you might choose to include dialogue about the strange Boo Radley, the dramatic Hallowe'en party and the trial of Tom Robinson.

Writing

Write a part for a narrator which appropriately links the two Jem and Scout dialogues.

You will need to decide who the narrator is to be. It could be Atticus, Jem, Scout or any other character from the book, or alternatively it could be a stage manager, the author or a reader of the book.

Drama

Use any of your writing in your drama. The letter from Atticus could provide another link in the scenes between Jem and Scout.

Shifting viewpoints of the reader

One helpful and interesting way of responding to a novel is to record your first impressions and then, at regular intervals:

Writing

As you begin your next novel, keep a log book in which you record your first impressions and then, at regular intervals:
■ comments about characters, the plot, style;
■ any uncertainties, lack of understanding, questions you would like to ask;
■ speculations about what is going to happen next;
■ any changes in your views about the story and the characters.

The use of diagrams to record development of plot and character and to mark the passing of time is recommended as another way of helping you to make links and organise your thoughts.

Talking

If two people or more are reading the same novel, it is a good idea to exchange impressions at agreed points in the story. This is especially helpful if you are engaged in reading a long novel such as *The Woman in White* by Wilkie Collins or *Jane Eyre* by Charlotte Brontë.

The reader as reviewer

Writing a review of a book provides the reader with an opportunity to:
■ reflect upon what has been read;
■ present a personal response;
■ consider a wider audience when assessing the merits of the book;
■ compare and contrast the book with others in the same genre.

Look at the two recent book reviews on pages 66 and 67.

The first is of *The Changeover* by Margaret Mahy. It is reviewed by Jacqui Hayden, aged 16, winner of the First Prize, Category B in *The Sunday Observer* competition, 1985.

FIRST PRIZE
Category B
Jacqui Hayden, 16, of Buckley, Clwyd reviewing 'The Changeover' by Margaret Mahy

When I first picked up 'The Changeover' I was unsure what to expect, for romances about teenagers written by adults are invariably stale and uninteresting.

Therefore, I was surprised to discover an exciting tale of the supernatural combined with the very human story of Laura Chant, facing the problems of approaching adulthood with trepidation. Margaret Mahy deals with the topic of teenage romance with delicacy and understanding.

Laura Chant suspects that she possesses dormant, supernat-ural powers, but it is only when her brother Jacko becomes mysteriously ill that she realises the extent of them. Only she knows that her brother's life source is slowly being drained away by the evil Carmody Braque.

In desperation Laura turns to the only person she believes can help her: Sorenson Carlisle. Although Laura has never spoken to the newcomer she recognises powers within him.

Together Laura and Sorry begin the battle against Carmody Braque; and as the story unfolds Laura finds herself trapped in a supernatural world, faced with the decision either to watch her brother die or to make a change which will alter her life forever. Laura makes her choice. She undergoes the 'changeover' and begins a cam-paign to rid the world of Carmody Braque.

'The Changeover' also tells of how Laura is forced to grow up suddenly when her mother's friend Chris Holly intrudes unexpectedly into the family home. But above all, the novel is about the love which blossoms between Sorry and Laura. In this captivating novel, Margaret Mahy's strong sense of reality prevents a potentially far-fetched story-line from becoming unreal. She manages, with originality of thought and expression, to create credible characters who, even at the height of supernatural drama, make the story totally believable.

This is the first of Margaret Mahy's books written exclusively for teenagers. I hope she writes many more.

Talking

What do you learn from Jacqui's review about:
■ the kind of story told in the book;
■ the main characters;
■ the theme of the book; and
■ her response to it?
Does her review make you want to read the book?

The second review is of *What is the Truth?* by Ted Hughes. It was written by Stephanie Nettell, one of the judges of the 'Guardian Children's Fiction Award', 1985.

The judges of this year's Guardian Children's Fiction Award felt that Ted Hughes's **What is the Truth?** (Faber, £7.95) stood alone as a very special children's work indeed. They would acknowledge at once that few young readers are likely to embark on it on their own, but with a sympathetic adult to point the way, what a truly marvellous range of pleasures it offers, what a wealth of rhyming and metrical forms, of imagery and language games, what vigour, what unexpectedness, what sadness, what fun. Imaginative teachers will fall on it.

Hughes has never forgotten the chance influence of his youth that revealed to him that he could write poetry, and much of his life's work – the Arvon schools and a broad shelf of books for children of all ages – has been determined by a conviction that everyone should be given that chance for contact and example. More than any other serious poet, he has consistently offered young people a body of writing, both prose and verse, that is demanding, and rigorous yet accessible, filtering his adult ferocity and physicality without trivialising or enfeebling it.

'What is the Truth?' is subtitled 'A Farmyard Fable For The Young', but the continuing question God's Son asks different members of a rural community through their dreams is finally answered more satisfyingly for young people by the cumulative suggestion that each creature, each person, is his or her own truth, that there is no one orthodox truth, than by the pantheistic declarations of God that 'I am the Rat. I am the Foal ... I am each of these things' – and in any case matters far less than the rich variety of the discarded answers the country people offer.

These come in 60 poems about familiar animals, from horses to fleas, viewed with affection or scorn, humour or pity, always with an extraordinary blend of poetic passion and absolute veracity – Hughes *knows* his animals. No town child will ever again look at a cat or a pigeon without actually seeing it, no country child take either buzzard or cow for granted.

But 'What is the Truth?' not only opens children's eyes and hearts to the wildlife around them, it shows them how they too can use language as a tool to manipulate, excite and explore feelings. Not only will children, after reading it, be looking at the world with a clearer, shrewder eye, but they too will want to write about their own animals and feelings. Here is that magical thing: a book to make writers as well as readers.

The reactions of the judges to the stylised tone drawings of the Devon artist, R. J. Lloyd, with which the book is heavily illustrated, ranged right through the spectrum, reflecting the current debate among those who work with children on whether poetry illustration should merely decorate, or be as dominant as the printed words. Lloyd's illustrations make a strong personal contribution to a big, handsome production, a work for young people to dip into, listen to, return to, mull over, and recollect years later with a shiver of recognition.

Talking and writing

- What do you learn from this article about the kind of book being reviewed and its author?
- 'Imaginative teachers will fall on it'. Why? List the claims made for the book as one to introduce to young readers.
- Choose either a book for young adults or one especially written for young children. Write a review which expresses a personal viewpoint and keeps in mind the wider audience for whom it is written, e.g. as an article for a school magazine or for display in a public library.

DRAMA

Roots, Arnold Wesker

There are several ways through which we can approach and make enjoyable the study of a set text. We have already introduced you to the idea of 'picking up clues' before you begin to read a novel, play or poem. Brainstorming and improvisation are two more methods you might try.

Brainstorming

Work in groups.

You will need a large sheet of paper and a pencil. Appoint one person to be responsible for receiving all the ideas in any order and for jotting them down. Remember this technique is successful within groups which:

- accept all ideas (quantity is more important than quality at this stage);
- do not criticise any person's contribution;
- are able to be open-minded about the subject under discussion;
- listen to individual contributions and build on the ideas expressed.

Now, do a 'Brainstorming' exercise on the word

ROOTS

Select one of the ideas which you think could be developed as
an interesting plot for a play.

Share your thinking with other groups.

You have been required constantly to shift your viewpoint
during the brainstorming activity; now we suggest you focus on
Beatie, the central character in this play.

[*There is a knock on the front door.*]

BEATIE   [*jumping down joyously as though her excited quotes have been
leading to this one moment*] He's here, he's here! [*But at the door it is
the* POSTMAN, *from whom she takes a letter and a parcel.*] Oh, the silly
fool, the fool. Trust him to write a letter on the day he's
coming. Parcel for you Mother.

PEARL   Oh, that'll be your dress from the club.

MRS BRYANT   What dress is this then? I didn't ask for no dress
from the club.

PEARL   Yes you did, you did ask me, didn't she ask me Frank?
Why, we were looking through the book together Mother.

MRS BRYANT   No matters what we was doin' together I aren't
hevin' it.

PEARL   But Mother you distinctly –

MRS BRYANT   I aren't hevin' it so there now!

[BEATIE *has read the letter – the contents stun her. She cannot move. She
stares around speechlessly at everyone.*]

MRS BRYANT   Well, what's the matter wi' you gal? Let's have a
read. [*Takes letter and reads contents in a dead flat but loud voice – as
though it were a proclamation*] 'My dear Beatie. It wouldn't really
work would it? My ideas about handing on a new kind of life
are quite useless and romantic if I'm really honest. If I were a
healthy human being it might have been all right but most of
us intellectuals are pretty sick and neurotic – as you have often
observed – and we couldn't build a world even if we were given
the reins of government – not yet any-rate. I don't blame you
for being stubborn, I don't blame you for ignoring every
suggestion I ever made – I only blame myself for encouraging
you to believe we could make a go of it and now two weeks of
your not being here has given me the cowardly chance to think
about it and decide and I –'

BEATIE   [*snatching letter*] Shut up!

MRS BRYANT   Oh – so we know now do we?

MR BRYANT   What's this then – ent he comin'?

MRS BRYANT   Yes, we know now.

MR BRYANT   Ent he comin' I ask?

BEATIE   *No he ent comin'.*

[*An awful silence ensues. Everyone looks uncomfortable.*]

JENNY   [*softly*] Well blust gal, didn't you know this was going to
happen?

[BEATIE *shakes her head.*]

MRS BRYANT So *we're* stubborn are we?

JENNY Shut you up Mother, the girl's upset.

MRS BRYANT Well I can see that, I can see that, he ent coming, I can see that, and we're here like bloody fools, I can see that.

PEARL Well did you quarrel all that much Beatie?

BEATIE [*as if discovering this for the first time*] He always wanted me to help him but I never could. Once he tried to teach me to type but soon ever I made a mistake I'd give up. I'd give up every time! I couldn't bear making mistakes. I don't know why, but I couldn't bear making mistakes.

MRS BRYANT Oh – so we're hearin' the other side o' the story now are we?

BEATIE He used to suggest I start to copy real objects on to my paintings instead of only abstracts and I never took heed.

MRS BRYANT Oh, so you never took heed.

JENNY Shut you up I say.

BEATIE He gimme a book sometimes and I never bothered to read it.

FRANK [*not maliciously*] What about all this discussion we heard of?

BEATIE I *never* discussed things. He used to beg me to discuss things but I never saw the point on it.

PEARL And he got riled because o' that?

BEATIE [*trying to understand*] I didn't have any patience.

MRS BRYANT Now it's coming out.

BEATIE I couldn't help him – I never knew patience. Once he looked at me with terrified eyes and said, 'We've been together for three years but you don't know who I am or what I'm trying to say – and you don't care do you?'

MRS BRYANT And there she was tellin' me.

BEATIE I never knew what he wanted – I didn't think it mattered.

MR BRYANT And there she were gettin' us to solve the moral problem and now we know she didn't even do it herself. That's a rum 'un, ent it?

MRS BRYANT The apple don't fall far from the tree – that it don't.

BEATIE [*wearily*] So you're proud on it? You sit there smug and you're proud that a daughter of yours wasn't able to help her boy friend? Look at you. All of you. You can't say anything. You can't even help your own flesh and blood. Your daughter's bin ditched. It's your problem as well isn't it? I'm part of your family aren't I? Well, help me then! Give me words of comfort! Talk to me – for God's sake, someone talk to me. [*She cries at last.*]

MR BRYANT Well, what do we do now?

MRS BRYANT We sit down and we eat that's what we do now.

JENNY Don't be soft Mother, we can't leave the girl crying like that.

MRS BRYANT Well, blust, 'tent my fault she's cryin'. I did what I could – I prepared all this food, I'd've treated him as my own son if he'd come but he hevn't! We got a whole family gathering specially to greet him, all on us look, but he hevn't come. So what am I supposed to do?

BEATIE   My God, Mother, I hate you – the only thing I ever
wanted and I weren't able to keep him, I didn't know how. I
hate you, I hate . . .

[MRS BRYANT *slaps Beatie's face. Everyone is a little shocked at this
harsh treatment.*]

MRS BRYANT   There! I hed enough!

MR BRYANT   Well what d'you wanna do that for?

MRS BRYANT   I hed enough. All this time she've bin home she've
bin tellin' me I didn't do this and I didn't do that and I hevn't
understood half what she've said and I've hed enough. She talk
about bein' part o' the family but she've never lived at home
since she've left school look. Then she go away from here and
fill her head wi' high-class squit and then it turn out she don't
understand any on it herself. It turn out she do just the same
things she say I do. [*Into Beatie's face*] Well, am I right gal? I'm
right ent I? When you tell me I was stubborn, what you mean
was that *he* told you *you* was stubborn – eh? When you tell me I
don't understand you mean *you* don't understand isn't it?
When you tell me I don't make no effort you mean *you* don't
make no effort. Well, what you blaming me for? Blaming me all
the time! I haven't bin responsible for you since you left home –
you bin on your own. She think I like it, she do! Thinks I like it
being cooped up in this house all day. Well I'm telling you my
gal – I don't! There! And if I had a chance to be away working
somewhere the whole lot on you's could go to hell – the lot on
you's. All right so I am a bloody fool – all right! So I know it! A
whole two weeks I've bin told it. Well, so then I can't help you
my gal, no that I can't, and you get used to that once and for
all.

BEATIE   No you can't Mother, I know you can't.

MRS BRYANT   I suppose doin' all those things for him weren't
enough. I suppose he weren't satisfied wi' goodness only.

BEATIE   Oh, what's the use.

MRS BRYANT   Well, don't you sit there an' sigh gal like you was
Lady Nevershit. I ask you something. Answer me. You do the
talking then. Go on – you say you know something we don't so
you do the talking. Talk – go on, talk gal.

BEATIE   [*despairingly*] I can't Mother, you're right – the apple
don't fall far from the tree do it? You're right, I'm like you.
Stubborn, empty, wi' no tools for livin'. I got no roots in
nothing. I come from a family o' farm labourers yet I ent got no
roots – just like town people – just a mass o' nothin'.

FRANK   Roots, gal? What do you mean, roots?

BEATIE   [*impatiently*] Roots, roots, roots! Christ, Frankie, you're
in the fields all day, you should know about growing things.
Roots! The things you come from, the things that feed you. The
things that make you proud of yourself — roots!

MR BRYANT   You got a family ent you?

BEATIE   I am not talking about family roots – I mean – the – I
mean – Look! Ever since it begun the world's bin growin'
hasn't it? Things hev happened, things have bin discovered,

people have bin thinking and improving and inventing but what do we know about it all?

JIMMY   What is she on about?

BEATIE   [*various interjections*] What do you mean, what am I on about? I'm talking! Listen to me! I'm tellin' you that the world's bin growing for two thousand years and we hevn't noticed it. I'm telling you that we don't know what we are or where we come from. I'm telling you something's cut us off from the beginning. I'm telling you we've got no roots. Blimey Joe! We've all got large allotments, we all grow things around us so we should know about roots. You know how to keep your flowers alive don't you Mother? Jimmy – you know how to keep the roots of your veges strong and healthy. It's not only the corn that need strong roots, you know, it's us too. But what've we got? Go on, tell me, what've we got? We don't know where we push up from and we don't bother neither.

PEARL   Well, I aren't grumbling.

BEATIE   You say you aren't – oh yes, you say so, but look at you. What've you done since you come in? Hev you said anythin'? I mean really said or done anything to show you're alive? Alive! Blust, what do it mean? Do you know what it mean? Any of you? Shall I tell you what Susie said when I went and saw her? She say she don't care if that ole atom bomb drop and she die – that's what she say. And you know why she say it? I'll tell you why, because if she had to care she'd have to do something about it and she find *that* too much effort. Yes she do. She can't be bothered – she's too bored with it all. That's what we all are – we're all too bored.

MRS BRYANT   Blust woman – bored you say, bored? You say Susie's bored, with a radio and television an' that? I go t'hell if she's bored!

BEATIE   Oh yes, we turn on a radio or a TV set maybe, or we go to the pictures – if them's love stories or gangsters – but isn't that the easiest way out? Anything so long as we don't have to make an effort. Well, am I right? You know I'm right. Education ent only books and music – it's asking questions, all the time. There are millions of us, all over the country, and no one, not one of us, is asking questions, we're all taking the easiest way out. Everyone I ever worked with took the easiest way out. We don't fight for anything, we're so mentally lazy we might as well be dead. Blust, we are dead! And you know what Ronnie say sometimes? He say it serves us right! That's what he say – it's our own bloody fault!

JIMMY   So that's us summed up then – so we know where *we* are then!

MRS BRYANT   Well if he don't reckon we count nor nothin', then it's as well he didn't come. There! It's as well he didn't come.

BEATIE   Oh, *he* thinks we count all right – living in mystic communion with nature. Living in mystic bloody communion with nature (indeed). But us count? Count Mother? I wonder. Do we? Do you think we really count? You don' wanna take any notice of what them ole papers say about the workers bein' all-important these days – that's all squit! 'Cos we aren't. Do you think when the really talented people in the country get to work they get to work for us? Hell if they do! Do you think they don't know we 'ont make the effort? The writers don't write thinkin' we can understand, nor the painters don't paint expecting us to be interested – that they don't, nor don't the composers give out music thinking we can appreciate it. 'Blust,' they say, 'the masses is too stupid for us to come down to them. Blust,' they say, 'if they don't make no effort why should we bother?' So you know who come along? The slop singers and the pop writers and the film makers and women's magazines and the Sunday papers and the picture strip love stories – that's who come along, and you don't have to make no effort for them, it come easy. 'We know where the money lie,' they say, 'hell we do! The workers've got it so let's give them what they want. If they want slop songs and film idols we'll give 'em that then. If they want words of one syllable, we'll give 'em that then. If they want the third-rate, *blust!* We'll give 'em *that* then. Anything's good enough for them 'cos they don't ask for no more!' The whole stinkin' commercial world insults us and we don't care a damn. Well, Ronnie's right – it's our own bloody fault. We want the third-rate – we got it! We got it! We got it! We . . .

[*Suddenly* BEATIE *stops as if listening to herself. She pauses, turns with an ecstatic smile on her face –*]

D' you hear that? D'you hear it? Did you listen to me? I'm talking. Jenny, Frankie, Mother – I'm not quoting no more.

MRS BRYANT [*getting up to sit at table*] Oh hell, I hed enough of her – let her talk a while she'll soon get fed up.

[*The others join her at the table and proceed to eat and murmur.*]

BEATIE Listen to me someone. [*As though a vision were revealed to her*] God in heaven, *Ronnie!* It does work, it's happening to me, I can feel it's happened, I'm beginning, on my own two feet – I'm beginning . . .

[*The murmur of the family sitting down to eat grows as* BEATIE*'s last cry is heard. Whatever she will do they will continue to live as before. As* BEATIE *stands alone, articulate at last –*]

THE CURTAIN FALLS

Reading aloud   Read through the extract. If you wish to attempt the Norfolk accent and intonation, the following guidelines may be of some help. The play could be about country people anywhere, so don't allow the accent to become a barrier to your understanding of character and plot.

'ing' words, e.g. doing, coming: lose the 'g', e.g. doin', comin'
having, have, had: hevin', hev, hed
isn't, it isn't, won't: ent, (short, sharp) 'tent, on't
'ee', e.g. been, seen: bin, sin
blast: blust
of it, **of us**: on it, on us
girl: gal

Form

One of the most interesting features about this scene is that Beatie seldom talks to anyone other than herself. Check this by reading her part only from 'He always wanted me to help him' to 'I didn't think it mattered'.

It is by writing 'speeches' for Beatie and using rhetorical questions, that Wesker emphasises her lack of communication with her family and her desire to find her 'own voice'.

Talking

What have you discovered from this extract about Beatie, her boyfriend and her life-style both before she came home and during the two weeks she has been home preparing her family to meet Ronnie?

What are the changes in Beatie's view of herself from the moment the letter arrives until the end of the scene? As you discuss, it will help you to plot the 'rise and fall' of her emotions by jotting down some key words and phrases from the text, e.g.

'He's here, he's here'
'the contents stun her'
'Shut up!'
'No he ent comin''

Discuss your feelings about the relationship between Beatie and her mother. Do your sympathies change during this scene? Where do you think the playwright's sympathies lie?

Pearl finds it extraordinary that Beatie's boyfriend was annoyed because Beatie could not discuss things with him. Do you find Ronnie's annoyance extraordinary?

Class activity

All playwrights, through their characters, express their views about life. In this extract what are the thoughts and feelings of Arnold Wesker about the following?
- Communication. 'We've been together for three years but you don't know who I am or what I am trying to say'.
- Education. 'Education ent only books and music – it's asking questions, all the time.'
- The commercial world. 'The whole stinkin' commercial world insults us and we don't care a damn.'

Take one of the above topics and discuss it in depth.

Collect information and examples from television programmes, newspapers, magazines, popular music, etc. to help you to decide whether the criticisms that Wesker was making about life for the masses in the 1960s are still true today.

Writing

Develop in writing any of the ideas which you have found interesting in your group discussions. Here are some suggestions which make use of different forms of writing.
- Look closely at Beatie's final speech. Use it as a model to write *a speech* on a topic about which you feel strongly. Use rhetorical questions, give examples to support and build up your point of view and end on a phrase which will clinch your argument and stay in the mind of the audience.

■ Write the letter which Beatie, as she is at the end of the play, might have written back to Ronnie.

Drama

Improvisation

Work in small groups.
■ Use the words 'I've had enough' at some important point in your improvisation of one of the following situations.
  — A family scene at a meal time during which one person, who has remained silent, suddenly breaks in with the words 'I've had enough'.
  — A family gathers after a funeral to hear the will. The dead person speaks the words 'I've had enough'.
  — An unemployed young person in the queue at the social security office interrupts the silence with the words 'I've had enough'.
■ Home for the Holidays! A student returns after an exciting first term at college. He or she tries to hold a conversation with friends whose interests and attitudes are now very different from his or hers.
■ A person has been in hospital for some considerable time. Her view of life has been restricted to that of a hospital ward. Visitors who come attempt to interest her in their activities . . . Develop the conversations between the patient and her visitors.
■ Use any of your writing or quotations from the play as starting points for further improvisations.
■ Ten years on . . . Improvise a scene in which Beatie once again returns home for a family reunion.

Reading

Read the whole play.

Further development

Select from all your work in talk, writing and drama, material which could be used in a short programme during which you introduce the play *Roots* to another 4th or 5th year group. You may decide to read extracts; to act out prepared improvisations of some of the themes; to hold a formal debate on one of the issues raised, etc. It will be interesting to see how another group reacts to the brainstorming of the word ROOTS.

4 Taking on a role and improvisation

You will have seen the words 'role play' and 'improvisation' many times in English and Drama course books and from the activities suggested or situations described, you probably have some idea of what it means to 'take on a role' and to 'improvise'.

Although we have asked you to adopt roles and work through improvisation in many other parts of the book, this chapter is particularly concerned with their value in helping you towards a deeper understanding of people, issues, problems and themes through literature we have chosen.

Taking on a role

A situation is described which you explore by taking one or several different viewpoints or attitudes, e.g. to take on the 'role' of an elderly person threatened with eviction is different from acting as if you were old Mrs Simpson herself, using appropriate voice, movements and gestures.

You will *not* be required to use acting skills but asked to use *talk* and maybe some movement to work your way through the problem presented to you.

Once you are 'in role' try to sustain it and avoid any temptation to involve 'teacher' in your dialogue unless she/he is also in role. 'Out of role' it is essential that you discuss as a group what you have learnt, the viewpoints you have shared, and whether your own attitude to the situation has in any way been developed or changed by the role-play experience.

Improvisation

Spontaneous improvisation is developing a drama as it is happening without the help of a script. It is more like everyday drama in the real world, where we respond to each other by picking up 'clues' which lead us to behave in one way or another. A simple example occurs when one person knocks on a door and someone else opens it.

Structured improvisation has, as the word suggests, more specific starting points, prescribed roles and an order in which events occur. Although the drama has a 'shape' from the start, those taking part are still free to develop their own roles and their relationships with each other. The 'outcome' of the situation being explored should never be decided upon before it happens.

Sometimes 'shaped' improvisations are rehearsed and 'polished' for presentation to an audience.

Writing down improvisations is one way of beginning to write a 'script'.

Improvisation

In pairs, improvise a situation in which:
- two men/women are unloading newspapers from vans;
- two travellers, strangers to each other, strike up a conversation;
- a policeman and a tramp are talking to each other;
- a station cleaner and a ticket collector talk together in the early hours of the morning;
- a newspaper reporter interviews a tramp for an article she is writing about the plight of London's homeless.

Talking

Think about and discuss what you have just been saying to each other in your improvisation(s). Ask yourselves some questions.
- How well did you pick up clues from each other as you talked?
- What did you learn about each other in role? Were there any marked contrasts between your two roles?
- Were there any 'uncomfortable' pauses? If there were how did you cope with them?
- Were your characters stereotypes or were you able to establish free-thinking individuals?
- Where and why did you decide to end your improvisation?

Writing

Script one of your dialogues and exchange it with another couple. Listen *critically* to your piece of work as it is presented and decide if any re-writing needs to be done.

VERSE

Tramps on Waterloo Station, Robert Morgan

It is 2 a.m. and I wait for a train out of London.
There is nothing to do but sit and wait
On the cold, darkened platform under clocks.
Newspaper vans unload news of governments,
Or Science and sex. There are men around me
Pretending to be travellers, passing time
Expertly in shadows and corners.
Some sleep with oblique heads on chests
Others embrace warm coffee machines
And stare and wait and ache with silence.
A man talks to himself quietly, facing
A wall and pointing at someone invisible.
As he moves from darkness to sanity he lifts
Up his head and sings an Irish song.
The notes unburden his eyeshut face
And a curved smile links him to a precious
Moment from the past. A man in rags
Lies in a heap on a bench in a bookshop shadow.

He uncurls himself like a tropical plant and
His face is a dark map of his life . . . confused,
Bitter, grimed, diseased, obsolete. . . .
My clean, modern clothes and full stomach
Remind me of my sanity and involvement with life.
But we are all moving towards the freedom
Of nonentity and they are the nearest to it.

Drama

Structured improvisation

Working as a class or in large groups, appoint a director to lead the discussion and plan the drama.

Read the poem with a view to exploring some or all of its images through role play and improvisation. It will help to consider the following questions as part of your preparation. Make notes for later use.

- How many different characters are mentioned in the poem?
- How is each one passing time?
- What snatch of song could the Irish tramp sing?
- What is the attitude of the poet towards the tramps? Is he sympathetic towards them or disgusted by them?
- Are there any other characters who would be likely to be on the platform at this time? Have you created any already in your improvisations which you could include in your drama?
- What simple props or costume could you make use of?

Use your notes to draw up a list of characters actually mentioned in the poem. Add any others for whom you have already written a dialogue.

Notice how the characters are seen by the poet as nameless and without identity, yet as he *focuses* his attention on each one he makes us briefly aware of that person's individuality.

How can you use information from the poem in order to establish character differences and movement in your improvisation?

Allow time for each 'character' or pair to take up a position in the acting area and to work on convincing movement and concentrated stillness.

Note to the director
As director, you will be in a position to move around the group, catching snatches of dialogue and observing the development of individual characters. Encourage the 'silent' tramps or travellers to assume a background and a reason for being on the station.

A powerful way of testing this out is for you to take on a role which gives you an opportunity to interact with each person or pair, e.g. the photographer accompanying the reporter; a welfare official looking for a missing person.

Polished improvisation

If you decide to share your group work with an audience, then you will need to decide:
- where the audience is in relation to your acting space;

- how you can control the dialogue so that not everyone is talking at once;
- whether to introduce any incident or movement which unites the group for a while; and
- how to end the drama.

Talking and writing

- Comment on the effectiveness of any of the work you have shared or been a part of.
- Write an evaluation of the work of your group. Include in your account a description of the group's improvisation and your contribution to it and your assessment of how successful you think your group was in using improvisation as a way of exploring themes in the poem.

Writing

- Basing your ideas on any in the poem or from discussion, write a scene which takes place on a railway station at different times of the day.
- Write the feature article for your newspaper based on the interview notes made on Waterloo Station. Choose an appropriate headline.

Further development

Writing

Use any ideas which have emerged from your talk, drama or writing as a starting point for a short story. Limit the number of characters, keep to one location and focus on one incident.

Improvisation

Focus on a situation in which a group of people pretend to be unknown to each other and are passing time hoping to go unnoticed by the authorities, e.g. escaped prisoners, spies, deserters from a pressure group.

DRAMA

The Children's Crusade, Paul Thompson

For two hundred years in the Middle Ages, Christian armies fought Muslims for possession of the Holy Land. These crusaders believed that the parts of Palestine where Jesus had lived should belong to them. At first they were successful; the first crusade ended with the capture of Jerusalem. The Muslims fought back, however, and by 1190 the Christians had been almost driven out of Palestine. From this time onwards, the conflict had less to do with religious ideals and more to do with political power and wealth. This was particularly true of the fourth crusade which, instead of going to Palestine, captured and looted the Christian cities of Zara and Constantinople.

The Children's Crusades were an angry response to this loss of spiritual idealism. In 1212 thousands of European children set out to win back the Holy Land by peaceful means. One crusade began in Vendôme in France, led by a twelve-year-old shepherd boy, Stephen de Cloyes; the second began in Germany six months later and it was led by a young boy called Nicholas, the hero of Paul Thompson's play. Nicholas was reputed to be gifted in the powers of speech and was encouraged by his father to organise an army of about thirty thousand children whose average age was probably fifteen.

Although rooted in history, Paul Thompson's play is contemporary in that it is about young people starting out with high ideals and expectations which later are shattered by the selfish and materialistic society in which they find themselves.

Reading

Here is the first extract taken from Act 1, Scene 2. Read it in groups.

FRANCIS   All who would follow Nicholas – step forward and take the vow! Join the Holy Crusade of Children!
[ONE BOY *steps forward and kneels before* NICHOLAS.]
NICHOLAS   [*swears in the first boy*] Do you promise to Christ Our Lord and to All the Saints, that you will fulfil the Sacred Task entrusted to you, that you will go to Jerusalem, that you will win the Cross?
BOY 1   I do.
NICHOLAS   Lord Jesus bless thy servant. Bless him and keep him safe always. – Amen. [ANOTHER BOY *steps forward. He kneels before* NICHOLAS.] [*Swears in the second boy.*] Do you promise to Christ Our Lord and to all the Saints, that you will fulfil the Sacred Task entrusted to you, that you will go to Jerusalem, that you will win the Cross?
BOY 2   I do.
NICHOLAS   Lord Jesus bless thy servant, bless him and keep him safe always. – Amen.
[*The vows ceremony continues as a silent mime. The ritualistic 'humming' continues.*]

['LEAVE-TAKINGS' – *These scenes should develop from improvisations.*]
[*Most of these scenes take place 'around' the town square, they could be lit by individual spotlights.*]

BOY *meets* GIRL.

JOHN   Is that Nicholas?
LESLEY   He's wonderful, isn't he?
JOHN   Are you going with him?
LESLEY   Yes.
JOHN   On your own? [*pause*] My name's John.

MOTHER *and two* SONS.

JANE   Goodbye, Martin.
COLIN   Goodbye, Mum.

JANE   Goodbye, Colin. Shall I say anything to your father?
MARTIN   No. Don't bother!

Two BROTHERS *and a* STRANGER

PATRICK   Look, here's another one . . . mugs!
TERRY   Is this the great gathering?
PATRICK   Here, are you going to walk through the water?
TERRY   We're going to Jerusalem, are you coming?
STEVE   Yeah.
PATRICK [*to* TERRY]   Push off.

Four SHOEMAKERS *at work overlooking the gathering*

PETER   Cor! look at that [*pause*]. Stuff this, let's go and join 'em.
ROSS   Yeah.
NIGEL [*to* RAY]   What do you say?
RAY   What about the guv'nor?
PETER   Sod the guv'nor. Where they're going there ain't no guv'nors.
RAY   No guv'nors? . . . That's marvellous.

Two SKYVERS

ANDREW   Are you going then?
TREVOR   No, too much walking.
ANDREW   It's better than working.
TREVOR   Yeah, that's a point.

Return to two BROTHERS – *'Walk through water'*

STEVE   Come on. Let's go!
PATRICK   No.
STEVE   Everyone else is going.
PATRICK   All right. Let's you and me walk through the water.

The COUNTRY BOY *and the* CITY BOY

MICHAEL   You're from the country, aren't you?
TONY   How did you know?
MICHAEL   You won't get far with no shoes. Why are you going?
TONY   No work. You?
MICHAEL   No jobs round here.

A MOTHER *says goodbye to her* DAUGHTER *and* SON

LINDY   It's a pilgrimage, it's not a war.
DEBBIE   I'm frightened.
LINDY   You've got your brother.
JONATHAN [*looking at* NICHOLAS]   We're with God.

The old CRUSADER *and two* BOYS

OLD CRUSADER   Look, lads, I'll tell you this for nothing. Don't go.
PAUL   It'll be different this time.

ROBERT   We're going in peace.

OLD CRUSADER   Yeah, I've heard that before – set out in peace, come home in pieces.

PAUL   Is that a joke?

OLD CRUSADER   I wish it was.

> JOE, *the late arrival, creeps into the square and kneels beside* two BROTHERS

JOE   I knew I'd be late. Ten days it took me to get here. I'm worn out before the journey starts.

NICK   Where do you come from?

JOE   Hamburg. You?

NICK   We live here.

JOE   You're lucky. Two hundred miles I've travelled. I'm knackered already.

SEBASTIAN   Do you want an apple?

JOE   Who's he?

NICK   My brother.

SEBASTIAN   I'm his brother.

JOE   Ta. [*He munches the apple.*]

NICHOLAS   Lord Jesus have mercy on us thy children. Give us thy blessing as we set out in thy service. Help us to be worthy of Thee.
[*The humming stops.*]

ALL   We promise to Christ Our Lord and to All the Saints, that we shall do His Holy will. That we shall live as He did live and go where He did go. We promise, unto *death*, that we shall fulfil the Sacred Task entrusted to us, that we shall go to Jerusalem, that we shall win the Cross.

NICHOLAS   Amen. [NICHOLAS's FATHER *approaches his son.*] Goodbye, father.

FATHER   Nicholas . . . the Lord be with you. [*They embrace.*] May God protect you.

NICHOLAS   He will father. He will.
[NICHOLAS *walks through the* CROWD. *They are still kneeling, they reach out to touch him. Music introduction.*]

You will notice that the children in this first scene are not developed as characters by the playwright; instead he has given his actors *roles* to play, e.g. 'Boy meets Girl', 'Mother and Two Sons', etc., which he suggests should be explored through *improvisation*.

Drama

Improvisation

Working in pairs or small groups, improvise a short scene in which you discuss whether or not to join Nicholas on the crusade. Each of you will need to give yourself a home, a background and a point of view about the crusade.

To help you to structure your improvisation sequence, we

suggest you build upon the playwright's ideas; you might consider using his dialogue as one way of ending your leave-taking scenes. Note the fact that the language used in these scenes is 'everyday' speech, in marked contrast to the language used in the 'vow-making' ceremony.

Work sharing

As you share your improvisations, take into account the following questions which are likely to be asked by a producer intending to incorporate them in the play.

- Are the improvisations imaginative, interesting, humorous as self-contained scenes?
- Do the pairs or groups have a good working relationship in which they show sympathetic interaction?
- Are the various roles within each improvisation scene sustained and developed?
- Is there sufficient variety and contrast when they are seen as a whole?

In the light of comments made, *polish* your improvisations until you are satisfied.

Decide on an order and a way of presenting the sequences. Possible links might be made using lighting, music or 'freeze' techniques.

One way of ending your presentation might be to include the 'vow-making' ceremony in which those young people who decide to accompany Nicholas are blessed by him. Use the words from the script 'Lord Jesus bless thy servant . . .' in the ceremony.

We have included a map of the crusaders' journey at this stage because it illustrates what an incredible journey it was. You might decide to represent it in dramatic terms as one way of signalling the *passage of time.*

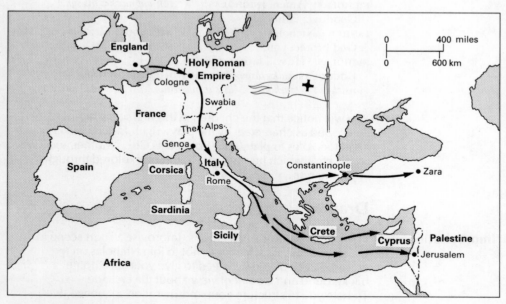

After much rejection and hardship, the children reach the city of
Genoa in Italy, where they see the sea for the first time. Nicholas
believes that their stay will be short; he expects the sea to divide
before them and allow them passage to Palestine. We take up the
action of the play at Scene 7 – the point where the Senators of
Genoa have called an emergency meeting of the Senate to
discuss the problem of a sudden influx of *thousands* of children.

The BISHOP OF GENOA *and* EIGHT SENATORS.

SENATOR 1   Senators, it's not a question of what we *want* to do,
it's a question of what we are *able* to do. This city just does not
have the facilities to cope with an influx of thousands of
children. To allow them to enter would precipitate a famine!

SENATOR 2   Rubbish!

SENATOR 1   I would normally choose to ignore that remark,
coming as it does, from such a worthless source. But this time
my ill-mannered friend has inadvertently pointed to yet
another problem. Rubbish. The problem of sanitation. These
children bring with them all kinds of diseases; they have been
on the road for months, in conditions which are beyond my
powers to describe. Many of them have died on the way . . .
and yet this house is seriously requested to debate the
possibility of permitting them to enter into our city. Senators, is
this how little you regard your city?

SENATOR 2   All you're concerned about is your purse. You've
done damn all for this city!

SENATOR 3   If you're so philanthropic – why don't you put 'em up
at your house?

SENATOR 2   Unlike you, my house is not so large and ostentatious
as to accommodate that many people.
[*Ad-lib.*]

BISHOP   Order . . . order!

SENATOR 1   It has been said that we have a duty to these
children. Well, that's as may be . . . certainly, they display
admirable courage and devotion to the Christian principle . . .
but I would remind this assembly that our primary duty is as it
always has been – to the citizens of Genoa. And in their name I
maintain that we would be failing in our duty if we allowed
these children to enter our city. Thank you.

SENATOR 4   We cannot forget that Frederick of Sicily is at war
with Otho of Germany, and in this conflict the City of Genoa is
aligned to the forces of Frederick through our devotion to His
Holiness Pope Innocent III.

SENATOR 6   What's that got to do with it?

SENATOR 2   Stand down, you fool.

SENATOR 4   It has everything to do with it! I would ask you to
consider, geographically, whereabouts this . . . 'Crusade' . . .
began. In Germany! Can we afford to overlook the possibility,
and I admit, it may only be a possibility . . . that these children

are emissaries from Otho – sent to capture our City!
[*General laughter.*]
You may laugh. You may laugh . . . but if my fears should prove to be well-founded . . . I hope you have prepared your answers for His Holiness the Pope!

SENATOR 2   I presume that contribution to the debate was intended as a joke!

SENATOR 4   You'll see if it's a joke in the morning. You'll see, when there are thousands of urchins, with blond hair, blue eyes, running up and down the streets of Genoa.[1]

SENATOR 2   We shall direct our attention to the real problem that lies ahead and ignore the flights of fancy so typical of the previous speaker.

SENATOR 4   You'll see!

SENATOR 2   In the morning these children, in their innocence are expecting the sea to open before them. May I suggest that when this miraculous occurrence fails to occur . . . we shall have a riot on our hands. And we should be well advised to make plans for that riot, now. Do we know how many of them there are?

SENATOR 4   Twenty thousand!

SENATOR 5   Four!

SENATOR 1   Seven thousand!

SENATOR 7   Thirty thousand!

SENATOR 6   To prevent a riot . . . surely we could provide them with ships?

SENATOR 1   Who can?

SENATOR 6   If the sea fails to open. We could make them an offer of transportation to . . . well to a port where they might be more welcome.

SENATOR 1   Who'd have them?

SENATOR 3   Who'd pay for the ships? . . . They've got no money. Are you going to pay for it?

BISHOP   Senators, senators . . . please! [*Pause.*] There are no ships available.
[*Silence.*]

SENATOR 5   If I may be permitted. I suggest that we look at this question *rationally* . . . Where's the profit? Could our city conceivably *gain* from this experience?

SENATOR 4   No!

SENATOR 2   Could you gain from it you mean!

SENATOR 5   Gentlemen, if the Pope were to give his blessing to this 'Pilgrimage'. And if He saw that Genoa was doing what little the city could afford in order to help them. Then is it not possible that He might consider some reward . . . shall we say in the form of Tax Relief! This could give us an enormous trading advantage over Venice!

SENATOR 2   Ridiculous! Such an argument contains so many 'ifs' and 'buts' that you may as well wish for the moon! . . . Indeed my distinguished friend is become – a lunatic! His greed's got the better of his reason!
[*Laughter.*]

BISHOP   Order! Order! I must ask the House to curb its laughter.
Time is short!

SENATOR 5   Time is money!

SENATOR 3   These children need to eat! They may well be dying
of starvation! . . . We cannot provide them with work, so even
the most unimaginative of you must surely see that crime will
be inevitable. I'm not talking about the occasional pickpocket,
a burglary here or there . . . I'm talking of crime on a
mammoth scale! . . . Huge gangs of organized criminals,
robbers, prostitutes, violence . . . the looting of public places
. . . rape! subversion!

SENATOR 4   Anarchy!

[*Pause.*]

SENATOR 3   Senators we would be criminals ourselves if we
allowed them anywhere near our beautiful city!

SENATOR 1 ⎫ Right. I've got two daughters!
SENATOR 4 ⎪ Hear! Hear! At last someone's talking sense!
SENATOR 5 ⎬ Property first! Property first!
SENATOR 2 ⎭ Do we know they're criminals? If they're hungry
                why don't we feed 'em?

SENATOR 1 ⎫ Sit down! Sit down!
SENATOR 4 ⎪ You've got nothing to lose!
SENATOR 5 ⎬ Who's going to pay the bill? Are you going to pay it?
SENATOR 8 ⎪ There must be another way of handling this.
BISHOP   ⎪ Order! Order! Order! Order! Order! Order!
SENATOR 7 ⎭ Senators! Please! Quiet!

[*Above the noise.*]

SENATOR 3   If anything goes wrong - we are the ones responsible!

---

[1] Author's Note – It must be made clear that the Senator is voicing his own
prejudices and fears rather than giving an accurate description of the members
of the cast. In fact the National Youth Theatre cast was multiracial.

Reading

Now, in groups, read scene seven again.

Just as the children in Scene 2 were given roles rather than
characters, so the senators are not named but are given roles in
which they represent *attitudes* towards the problem raised in this
scene.

Drawing

One helpful way of making a study of one role in relation to
another is to record information in simple diagrams.
    Using our example on page 86, draw and complete a 'box' for
each Senator.

Senator	Attitudes	Key Quotations
?	Materialistic	'Where's the profit?' 'Property first! Property first!' 'Time is money!'
1	Practical, resistant to change, cynic	?
?	?	'You'll see, when there are thousands of urchins, with blond hair, blue eyes, running up and down the streets of Genoa.'

When you have completed your diagram you will see that, with such entrenched attitudes, it is unlikely that this group of senators would ever be able to solve any problem! They *are* the problem! But given a similar situation today we wonder whether the same attitudes might be expressed.

Talking

Working in groups, consider a situation in which a committee has to meet to discuss
■ a request for aid;
■ a plan for redevelopment; or
■ an application for permission to hold a festival of pop music in the vicinity.
After deciding which issue to tackle, fill in the details so that you all have a common basis for discussion. Elect a chairperson.

Writing

Each person in the group should adopt a role (attitude) towards the chosen problem. Write notes expressing your viewpoint. Underline 'key' phrases which you are determined to use when the committee meets.

Improvisation

Act out your 'committee scene'. Tape record it if possible.

Writing

Working individually or in pairs now, script your own scene. Make use of your notes, key phrases and your tape recording.

You won't be able to use all the conversation, but make sure that all the different attitudes are represented.

Refer to Scene 7 from *The Children's Crusade* to help you to *shape* your writing with an audience in mind.

NOVEL

Animal Farm, George Orwell

'Role play' and improvisation provide exciting opportunities for:
■ preparation before a first reading of a book;
■ exploring characters, issues and themes during, as well as

after, the reading;
- focusing on individual parts of the novel, which might help to a clearer understanding of the whole;
- a refreshing and effective way of revising a book before an examination;
- using other stories, plays and poems concerned with similar themes;
- introducing the book in an interesting way to other groups of students.

Animal Farm by George Orwell is one story with which many of you will already be familiar and might be studying as a set book. It is from this book that we have chosen examples to show this way of working.

Talking and drama

Working in groups, talk about the skills needed to make a person effective as a public speaker. Give examples of any people you admire who have the qualities mentioned.

Choose one person prepared to be the spokesperson for the group and help that person to prepare a short speech on *one* of the following topics, or any other topic of your own choosing.
- Shorter School Hours – Shorter Holidays
- The Abolition of Public Examinations
- All Women Are Equal

Talk through and jot down quickly the main points of your group's speech.

Rehearse your speaker in preparation for a public meeting. Here are a few helpful hints.
- Command attention by standing confidently; assume a 'presence' on the platform. Use gesture when appropriate. Speak clearly.
- Use pause for dramatic emphasis.
- Sustain the argument despite likely opposition from voices in the crowd.
- Refer to notes in as natural a manner as possible; always *read* quotations.
- Establish and maintain eye contact with the audience.

Now, working as a whole class, role play a situation in which you all are the audience for each of the appointed speakers.

Evaluation

Ask yourself the following questions.
- Did you support your 'own' speaker? How?
- Did you change your opinion about any of the issues as they were presented?
- Did you speak? Were you pleased with your 'performance'?
- Were you influenced by *who* was speaking rather than by *what* was being said?

During your reading of the novel you will find many examples when public speaking is used to inspire, inform, inflame and persuade.

In chapter one, old Major, the prize boar on Manor Farm, calls all the animals together to tell them of his dream of the earth as it would be when man had vanished. At the end of the speech in which his aim is to inspire them to overthrow Jones, the owner, he concludes:

'I have little more to say. I merely repeat, remember always your duty of enmity towards Man and all his ways. Whatever goes upon two legs, is an enemy. Whatever goes upon four legs, or has wings, is a friend. And remember also that in fighting against Man, we must not come to resemble him. Even when you have conquered him, do not adopt his vices. No animal must ever live in a house, or sleep in a bed, or wear clothes, or drink alcohol, or smoke tobacco, or touch money, or engage in trade. All the habits of Man are evil. And, above all, no animal must ever tyrannize over his own kind. Weak or strong, clever or simple, we are all brothers. No animal must ever kill any other animal. All animals are equal.

Three nights later, old Major died. During the following months, the pigs emerged as natural leaders and:

Pre-eminent among the pigs were two young boars named Snowball and Napoleon, whom Mr Jones was breeding up for sale. Napoleon was a large, rather fierce-looking Berkshire boar, the only Berkshire on the farm, not much of a talker, but with a reputation for getting his own way. Snowball was a more vivacious pig than Napoleon, quicker in speech and more inventive, but was not considered to have the same depth of character. All the other male pigs on the farm were porkers. The best known among them was a small fat pig named Squealer, with very round cheeks, twinkling eyes, nimble movements, and a shrill voice. He was a brilliant talker, and when he was arguing some difficult point he had a way of skipping from side to side and whisking his tail which was somehow very persuasive. The others said of Squealer that he could turn black into white.

These three had elaborated old Major's teachings into a complete system of thought, to which they gave the name of Animalism. Several nights a week, after Mr Jones was asleep, they held secret meetings in the barn and expounded the principles of Animalism to the others. At the beginning they met with such stupidity and apathy. Some of the animals talked of the duty of loyalty to Mr Jones, whom they referred to as 'Master', or made elementary remarks such as 'Mr Jones feeds us. If he were gone, we should starve to death.' Others asked such questions as 'Why should we care what happens after we are dead?' or 'If this rebellion is to happen anyway, what difference does it make whether we work for it or not?', and the pigs had great difficulty in making them see that this was contrary to the spirit of Animalism. The stupidest questions of all were asked by Mollie, the white mare. The very first question she asked Snowball was: 'Will there still be sugar after the Rebellion?'

Handwritten annotations:
windmill idea
"good-looking?".
doesn't pig
evil
useful!
but then changes through the book to Napoleon's views.
Mr Jones is an evil man but the animals think he is good because he feeds them.
stupid character

'No,' said Snowball firmly. 'We have no means of making sugar on this farm. Besides, you do not need sugar. You will have all the oats and hay you want.'

'And shall I still be allowed to wear ribbons in my mane?' asked Mollie.

'Comrade', said Snowball, 'those ribbons that you are so devoted to are the badge of slavery. Can you not understand that liberty is worth more than ribbons?'

Mollie agreed, but she did not sound very convinced.

Vain

sounds like a proper rebellion

At regular meetings everyone had a chance to discuss and vote on future plans. The only disagreements took place between Snowball and Napoleon; the first one was to do with 'selective education'.

Napoleon took no interest in Snowball's committees. He said that the education of the young was more important than anything that could be done for those who were already grown up. It happened that Jessie and Bluebell had both whelped soon after the hay harvest, giving birth between them to nine sturdy puppies. As soon as they were weaned, Napoleon took them away from their mothers, saying that he would make himself responsible for their education. He took them up into a loft which could only be reached by a ladder from the harness-room, and there kept them in such seclusion that the rest of the farm soon forgot their existence.

The mystery of where the milk went to was soon cleared up. It was mixed every day into the pigs' mash. The early apples were now ripening, and the grass of the orchard was littered with windfalls. The animals had assumed as a matter of course that these would be shared out equally; one day, however, the order went forth that all the windfalls were to be collected and brought to the harness-room for the use of the pigs. At this some of the other animals murmured, but it was no use. All the pigs were in full agreement on this point, even Snowball and Napoleon. Squealer was sent to make the necessary explanation to the others.

'Comrades!' he cried. 'You do not imagine, I hope, that we pigs are doing this in a spirit of selfishness and privilege? Many of us actually dislike milk and apples. I dislike them myself. Our sole object in taking these things is to preserve our health. Milk and apples (this has been proved by Science, comrades) contain substances absolutely necessary to the well-being of a pig. We pigs are brain-workers. The whole management and organization of this farm depend on us. Day and night we are watching over your welfare. It is for *your* sake that we drink that milk and eat those apples. Do you know what would happen if we pigs failed in our duty? Jones would come back! Yes, Jones would come back! Surely, comrades,' cried Squealer almost pleadingly, skipping from side to side and whisking his tail, 'surely there is no one among you who wants to see Jones come back?'

Now if there was one thing that the animals were completely certain of, it was that they did not want Jones back. When it was put to them in this light, they had no more to say. The importance of keeping the pigs in good health was all too obvious. So it was agreed without further argument that the milk and the windfall apples (and also the main crop of apples when they ripened) should be reserved for the pigs alone.

The second major disagreement was over Snowball's plans to make modern labour-saving machinery.

At last the day came when Snowball's plans were completed. At the Meeting on the following Sunday the question of whether or not to begin work on the windmill was to be put to the vote. When the animals had assembled in the big barn, Snowball stood up and, though occasionally interrupted by bleating from the sheep, set forth his reasons for advocating the building of the windmill. Then Napoleon stood up to reply. He said very quietly that the windmill was nonsense and that he advised noboby to vote for it, promptly sat down again; he had spoken for barely thirty seconds, and seemed almost indifferent as to the effect he produced. At this Snowball sprang to his feet, and shouting down the sheep, who had begun bleating again, broke into a passionate appeal in favour of the windmill. Until now the animals had been about equally divided in their sympathies, but in a moment Snowball's eloquence had carried them away. In glowing sentences he painted a picture of Animal Farm as it might be when sordid labour was lifted from the animals' backs. His imagination had now run far beyond chaff-cutters and turnip-slicers. Electricity, he said, could operate threshing machines, ploughs, harrows, rollers, and reapers and binders, besides supplying every stall with its own electric light, hot and cold water, and an electric heater. By the time he had finished speaking, there was no doubt as to which way the vote would go.

To restore confidence amongst the animals and ensure support for Napoleon, the propagandist, Squealer, is sent on his mission.

'Comrades,' he said, 'I trust that every animal here appreciates the sacrifice that Comrade Napoleon has made in taking this extra labour upon himself. Do not imagine, comrade, that leadership is a pleasure! On the contrary, it is a deep and heavy responsibility. No one believes more firmly than Comrade Napoleon that all animals are equal. He would be only too happy to let you make your decisions for yourselves. But sometimes you might make the wrong decisions, comrades, and then where should we be? Suppose you had decided to follow Snowball, with his moonshine of windmills – Snowball, who, as we now know, was no better than a criminal?'

'He fought bravely at the Battle of the Cowshed,' said somebody.

'Bravery is not enough,' said Squealer. 'Loyalty and obedience are more important. And as to the Battle of the Cowshed, I believe the time will come when we shall find that Snowball's part in it was much exaggerated. Discipline, comrades, iron discipline! That is the watchword for today. One false step, and our enemies would be upon us. Surely, comrades, you do not want Jones back?'

Once again this argument was unanswerable. Certainly the animals did not want Jones back; if the holding of debates on Sunday mornings was liable to bring him back, then the debates must stop. Boxer, who had now had time to think things over, voiced the general feeling by saying: 'if Comrade Napoleon says it, it must be right'. And from then on he adopted the maxim, 'Napoleon is always right,' in addition to his private motto of 'I will work harder.'

The Voice in the Crowd

After only three weeks, Napoleon announced that, after all, the windmill was to be built and of course he sent Squealer (who 'could turn black into white') to tell the animals of this change of plan.

That evening Squealer explained privately to the other animals that Napoleon had never in reality been opposed to the windmill. On the contrary, it was he who had advocated it in the beginning, and the plan which Snowball had drawn on the floor of the incubator shed had actually been stolen from among Napoleon's papers. The windmill was, in fact, Napoleon's own creation. Why, then, asked somebody, had he spoken so strongly against it? Here Squealer looked very sly. That, he said, was Comrade Napoleon's cunning. He had *seemed* to oppose the windmill, simply as a manoeuvre to get rid of Snowball, who was a dangerous character and a bad influence. Now that Snowball was out of the way, the plan could go forward without his interference. This, said Squealer, was something called tactics. He repeated a number of times, 'Tactics, comrades, tactics!' skipping round and whisking his tail with a merry laugh. The animals were not certain what the word meant, but Squealer spoke so persuasively, and the three dogs who happened to be with him growled so threateningly, that they accepted his explanation without further questions.

Improvisation

Working in groups and using all the information available to you from any of the extracts, jot down any questions you might ask Napoleon, Snowball and Squealer if they were on trial. Three people are needed to role-play these characters and should spend time preparing their defence whilst the rest of the group prepare the questions they are going to ask. Here are some examples.

Snowball Why did you allow yourself to be driven off the farm?

Napoleon Did you never consider the possibility of forming an alliance with Snowball?

Squealer What did you mean when you said 'Bravery is not enough, loyalty and obedience are more important'.

If you are familiar with the novel, then you will be able to ask questions in the role of one of the characters.

Now conduct the trial scene.

One interesting further development might be to set an improvisation in the present day as follows.

The time is 1986. A firm is planning a campaign to introduce a new product into its range.

The managing director, about to retire, calls his employees together to tell them of his hopes for the future of the company if the product is a success and target dates are met.

Continue with this idea which might include grappling with

such issues and conflicts as:

- secret meetings called by the union representative who wants equal shares for all the work force;
- the choosing of a brand name and a slogan for the launching of the product;
- the training of salespeople on how to 'reach the public';
- a power struggle on the board of directors which leads to the workers voting;
- the use of propaganda techniques and bribes;
- an interviewer from radio coming to the firm to talk to the management and to ask the workers about their involvement with the product.

5　Focus on dialogue

Red Shift, Alan Garner

One decision that we have to make when writing a story is whether to write in the first or the third person; another is whether and when to include dialogue.

Many young writers, on having their work returned, will have read remarks such as 'I can't really believe that she would say that' or 'too much uninteresting conversation' or 'your dialogue does not develop your characters or further the action in your story'.

There is a strong temptation to use dialogue in the belief that it is easier to handle than narrative. In fact the ability to write convincing dialogue appropriately, requires considerable skill and practice. Good prose and credible dialogue develop best in a writer who has learned to be a good listener, and who is prepared to take the trouble to make it sound natural to the reader.

Alan Garner is one of the most skilful and challenging writers of our time and *Red Shift* is perhaps his most complex novel.

Alderley Edge in Cheshire is the setting for the novel in which Alan Garner uses shifting viewpoints, flashback techniques and the symbol of an axe head to weave together three narratives – a legend, an historical event and a modern love story.

This extract is concerned with the young lovers, Tom and Jan, and their finding of the axe head.

The road was steep, too steep to ride. The mountain was scattered with houses, but the village was at the top, gritstone cottages lodged among crags. The crags were grotesque. Cliffs, needles and slabs overhung the air, and in between were the houses, clamped to the rock. Dead quarries had sculpted the summit, and on the pinnacle stood a round tower and an arch, as if left from a great building, where no finished building could ever have been. The folly castle.

Tom and Jan parked their bicycles and climbed. The tilted slabs were polished by the wind.

'It's fantastic!' shouted Jan.

'Terrific!'

The wind scoured and cleansed. Inside the castle was hollow, with no stairs.

'Are you cold?' said Tom.

'No. I can feel it, but I'm not cold.'

To the north and east the Pennines led away. West and south

was the plain, and Wales beyond.

'This is us,' said Tom. 'This is honest. Down there, in that sludge, all the filth, all the problems. We're free of them.'

'Are we?'

'No, but it's a good image.'

'Barthomley and Crewe are down there, as well as the caravans.'

'Down there, up here: it doesn't matter as long as we know. Mow Cop just coincides with the difference.'

'Difference?'

'Between us up here and them down there.'

'Are you saying you're superior?'

'Different.' Tom stood outside the castle, on the cliff edge. 'This is for us.' Jan's hair blew across his face.

'Be careful.'

'Clean wind and the smell of your hair. I can't stand heights. Strange.'

They ate their sandwiches in a roofless cottage that was a filter for the wind. No more than collapsed walls and a fragment of gable were left.

'Fabulous, marvellous place,' said Tom. 'And us. Living. Breathing in and out: stupendous.'

'I wonder how many people have come home here,' said Jan. 'How many babies. How many fires have been lit. How much of everything.'

'And before that,' said Tom. They lay by the hearth. He reached up to the stone of the lintel. 'Millstone grit. It was a delta from a river that wore away mountains above Norway, not two spins of the galaxy ago. And before that?'

'I can't,' said Jan. 'It loses me. I stay with people. I love you.'

'Rudheath and the Rector had better start worrying soon,' said Tom.

'I know.'

He stroked her hair.

'But not yet,' said Jan.

'I know.'

'You don't mind.'

'I hope I wouldn't be so crass.'

'I love you,' said Jan.

'Tom's a-cold.'

'Are you?'

'I'm not cold. I said Tom's a-cold.'

'Good.'

'There's something in the chimney.'

'Don't move,' said Jan. 'It's our house.'

'That's all I grudge,' said Tom. 'Being skint doesn't matter – but if we could let rip, just one time. Just a few hours without worry about money.'

'I'm happy now,' said Jan. 'This will do me.'

'But one day,' said Tom, 'we shall.'

'One day. You're right: there is something in the chimney. It's smooth.'

Jan knelt on the fallen rubbish that blocked the hearth. 'It's cemented in. I can't move it. Be careful.'

'I'll take away the other stones round it,' said Tom. The mortar was perished, and he lifted the blocks away from the chimney breast. 'It's a cavity. Here she comes —'

'It's beautiful!'

Tom brushed the dirt with his sleeve. He held a stone axe head. It filled his palm. He rubbed with wet grass, and the axe shone grey-green, polished, flawless. It tapered to a thin edge at one end, and the other was a hammer shape, pierced for hafting.

'It's very beautiful,' said Tom.

'Let me hold it.' Jan took it as if it were a delicate bird. 'This is it,' she said. 'This is it. My real and special thing. Can we keep it? From our house?'

'Why not? A momentum of our visit. I doubt if the owner's still interested,' said Tom. 'But I am. Why wall it in?'

'A Bunty,' said Jan. 'A real thing.' She started to cry.

'What's the matter?'

'I love you. I'm so happy.'

'Crying?'

'I couldn't have pets, with moving, and dolls weren't real, and Mummy wasn't in, and when they were they were always busy or too tired, and we never made friends with moving, and I was so lonely, so alone, till you. I'd nothing till you. Nothing stayed. But you did. You rode those bikes. You came. You've never let anybody down. And now. We found it in our real house. We'll take turns to look after it, then we'll never be apart: this in your hand.'

'Orion,' said Tom. He held her. 'There's no end to you. I thought I had you worked out. I hadn't begun.'

'My face is a mess.'

'Your face is the most important thing I've ever seen.'

'I'm crying again.'

'So am I.'

The bicycles flew down Mow Cop. They passed Barthomley in darkness. Their lamps wove on the hills. Crewe was a glowing sky.

Tom handed the axe to Jan.

'Hello.'

'Hello.'

Reading aloud

In pairs, read the extract several times so that you are able to 'speak' the dialogue unselfconsciously and as naturally as possible.

Talking and writing

Now that you are more familiar with the passage, look at it again to evaluate its success in meeting the requirements set out in the first checklist below which concentrates on *character*.

Character: Dialogue should:
■ appear to be natural and appropriate;

■ give a clearer picture of the characters;
■ be punctuated in such a way that the reader knows exactly who is speaking;
■ show what the relationship is between the speakers;
■ indicate any differences between characters, e.g. from the way in which they speak as well as their attitudes towards the topic of conversation;
■ reflect the different emotions as they are being felt by the speakers; and
■ add to the sense of where the characters are and what they are doing.

Jot down examples from the dialogue between Tom and Jan which seem to fit any of the above criteria.

Attempt a 'first draft' piece of dialogue between two characters. In a short paragraph let your reader know where the characters are and what they are doing and then make your dialogue flow naturally from it. Remember that you are not writing a play script. A story isn't a play without stage directions.

Ask someone to read your work and be prepared to redraft any parts of it in response to helpful comments from your reader.

STORY

The Skylight, Penelope Mortimer

In this extract, a mother and her five-year-old son arrive at a house in France which they are going to rent, only to find it deserted and locked, with shutters over the windows. They find a ladder and an open skylight in the roof, but it is too small for the mother to climb through. Remembering that only a few weeks before, the little boy had locked himself in the lavatory and then, following her instructions, had managed to open the door, she invites him to climb the ladder, get inside the house and open one of the shuttered windows.

After explaining carefully what he is to do, and hiding her own anxiety, she lowers him through the skylight.

For the last time, she beat on the shutters, her blows as puny as his would have been. It was three hours since she had lowered him through the skylight. What more could she do? There was nothing more she could do. At last she said to herself, something has happened to him, I must go for help.

It was terrible to leave the house. As she stumbled down the steps and across the grass, which cut into her foot like stubble, she kept looking back, listening. Once she imagined she heard a cry, and ran back a few yards. But it was only the cicada.

It took her a long time to reach the road. The moon had risen. She walked in little spurts, running a few steps, then faltering, almost loitering until she began to run again. She remembered the pink house in the vineyard. She did not know how far it was; only that it was before the woods. She was crying all the time now, but did not notice it, any more than she was aware of her curious, in fact alarming, appearance. 'Johnny!' she kept sobbing, 'Oh, Johnny.' She began to trot, keeping up an even pace. The road rose and fell; over each slope she expected to see the lights of the pink house. When she saw the headlamps of a car bearing down on her she stepped into the middle of the road and beat her arms up and down, calling, 'Stop! Stop!'

The car swerved to avoid her, skidded, drew up with a scream across the road. She ran towards it.

'Please! . . . Please!. . .'

The faces of the three men were shocked and hostile. They began to shout at her in French. Their arms whirled like propellers. One shook his fist.

'Please. . .' she gasped, clinging to the window. 'Do you speak English? Please do you speak English?'

One of the men said, 'A little.' The other two turned on him. There was uproar.

'Please, I beg of you. It's my little boy.' Saying the words, she began to weep uncontrollably.

'An accident?'

'Yes, yes. In the house, up there. I can't get into the house –'

It was a long, difficult time before they understood; each amazing fact had to be interpreted. If it had been their home, they might have asked her in; at least opened the door. She had to implore and harangue them through a half-open window. At last the men consulted together.

'My friends say we cannot . . . enter this house. They do not wish to go to prison.'

'But it's *my* house – I've paid for it!'

'That may be. We do not know.'

'Then take me to the police – take me to the British Consul –'

The discussions became more deliberate. It seemed that they were going to believe her.

'But how can we get in? You say the house is locked up. We have no tools. We are not –'

'A hammer would do – if you had a hammer and chisel –'

They shook their heads. One of them even laughed. They were now perfectly relaxed, sitting comfortably in their seats. The interpreter lit a cigerette.

'There's a farm back there,' she entreated. 'It's only a little way. Will you take me? Please, please, will you take me?'

The interpreter considered this, slowly breathing smoke, before even putting it to his friends. He looked at his flat, black-faced, illuminated watch. Then he threw the question to them out of the corner of his mouth. They made sounds of doubt, weighing the possibility, the inconvenience.

'Johnny may be dying,' she said. 'He must have fallen. He must be hurt badly. He may,' her voice rose, she shook the window – 'he may be dead. . .'

They opened the back door and let her into the car.

'Turn round,' she said, 'it's back there on the left. But it's away from the road, so you must look out.'

In the car, since there was nothing she could do, she began to shiver. She realized for the first time her responsibility. *I may have murdered him.* The feeling of the child as she lifted him through the skylight came back to her hands: his warmth. The men, embarrassed, did not speak.

'There it is! There!'

They turned off the road. She struggled from the car before it had stopped, and ran to the front door. The men in the car waited, not wishing to compromise themselves, but curious to see what was going to happen.

The door was opened by a small woman in trousers. She was struck by a barrage of words, stepped back from it. Then, with her myopic eyes, she saw the whole shape of distress – a person in pieces. 'My dear,' she said. 'My dear . . . what's happened? What's the matter?'

*

Now there were so many people. The hours of being alone were over. But she did not speak. She sat forward on the seat, her hands tightly clasped, her face shrivelled. When they came to the turning she opened her lips and took a breath, but Miss Jardine had already directed them. They lurched and bumped up the lane, screamed to a stop, in front of the black barn doors.

'Is that locked too?' Yvonne asked.

There was no answer. They clambered out. Yvonne gave the tools and the rope to the men. Yvonne and Miss Jardine carried the blankets and the first-aid box. The moonlight turned the grass into lava.

'A torch,' Miss Jardine said, 'Blast!'

'We have a light,' the interpreter said, 'Although it does not seem necessary.'

'Good. Then let's go.'

She ran in front of them, although there was no purpose in reaching the house first. It was so clear in the moonlight that she could see the things spilled out of her handbag, the mirror of her powder compact, the brass catch of her purse. Before she was up the steps she began to call again, 'Johnny? Johnny?' The others, coming more slowly behind her with their burdens, felt pity, reluctance and dread.

'What shall we try first? The door?'

'No, we'll have to break a window. The door's too solid.'

'Which of you can use an axe?'

The men glanced at each other. Finally, the interpreter shrugged his shoulders and took the axe, weighing it. Yvonne spoke contemptuously to him, making as though to take the axe herself. He went up to the window, raised the axe and smashed it into the shutters. Glass and wood splintered. It had only needed one blow.

She was at the window, tugging at the jagged edges of the glass.

The interpreter pushed her out of the way. He undid the catch of the window and stood back, examining a small scratch on his wrist and shaking his hand in the air as though to relieve some intolerable hurt. She was through the window, blundering across a room, while she heard Miss Jardine calling, 'Open the front door if you can! Hold on! We're coming!'

They did not exist for her any longer. She did not look for light switches. The stairs were brilliant.

'Johnny?' she called. 'Johnny? Where are you?'

A door on the first-floor landing was wide open. She ran to the doorway and her hands, without any thought from herself, flew out and caught the lintel on either side, preventing her entrance.

He was lying on the floor. He was lying in exactly the same position in which he had curled on the grass outside, except that his thumb had fallen from his mouth; but it was still upright, still wet. His small snores came rhythmically, with a slight click at the end of each snore. Surrounding him was a confusion, a Christmas of toys. In his free hand he had been holding a wooden soldier; it was still propped inside the lax, curling fingers. She was aware, in a moment of absolute detachment, that the toys were very old; older, possibly, than herself. Then she stopped thinking. She walked forward.

Kneeling, she touched him. He mumbled, but did not wake up. She shook him, quite gently. He opened his eyes directly on to her awful, hardly recognizable face.

'I like the toys,' he said. His thumb went back into his mouth. His eyelids sank. His free hand gripped the soldier, then loosened.

'*Jonathan!*'

With one hand she pushed him upright. With the other, she hit him. She struck so hard that her palm stung.

One of the women started screaming, 'Oh, no! . . . No!'

She struggled to her feet and pushed past the blurred, obstructing figures in the doorway. She stumbled down the stairs. The child was crying. The dead house was full of sound. She flung herself into a room. 'Oh, thank God,' she whispered. 'Oh, thank God . . .' She crouched with her head on her knees, her arms wrapped round her own body, her body rocking with the pain of gratitude.

Talking and writing

After you have read the extract, read it once more with the following checklist in mind. This time the focus is on the relationship between dialogue and *style* and *plot*.

Style and *Plot*:   Dialogue should:
■ carry the action forward;
■ create variety and interest;
■ not attempt to 'imitate' accent; it is better to indicate in the narrative that a person is speaking with a strong regional or foreign accent;
■ flow out of the narrative and not attempt 'to say' everything that a character would say in a real life situation (i.e. be selective);

■ when used to convey essential information, do so briefly and
  have some element of surprise in it;
■ contribute to the overall shape and pace of the story;
■ sometimes be used to express 'relief' and humour as well as to
  create moments of tension at certain points in the story.

Look closely at:
■ the *dialogue* and find examples which meet the criteria set out
  in the checklist;
■ the *narrative* and find examples which show how it is used to
  reinforce the dialogue and to describe the thoughts and
  feelings of the mother, e.g. 'They began to shout at her in
  French. Their arms whirled like propellers.'

Either:
write the first part of this story as you imagine it would be from
when they arrive at the house to the point at which the mother
goes for help,
or,
write a story in which a person is alone. At some point in the
story it becomes necessary for your character to seek help. Use
The Skylight as your model to help you to write convincing
dialogue and to convey the rising tension through narrative.

Share your first draft with another person who will give you
constructive advice. Look back at both checklists for guidance in
employing dialogue.

VERSE

The Death of the Hired Man, Robert Frost

We are now so used to the long story being told in prose that we
tend to forget that, until the middle of the nineteenth century,
virtually all imaginative writing in England was in verse form.

It was the rise in popularity and respectability of the novel
which led poets to accept that the prose form was better suited to
the telling of long, complex stories than the poetic form.

The major nineteenth century poets, Byron, Browning,
Tennyson and Arnold, were some of the last to write long
narrative poems and dramatic monologues.

Although few long narrative poems continued to be written
after the mid-nineteenth century, there are many notable
exceptions. The American poet, Robert Frost, has written a
number of excellent poems in this form.

Louis Untermeyer introduces us to *The Death of the Hired
Man*, a poem which he describes as both a dialogue and a
drama.

'The Death of the Hired Man' is many kinds of poem. It is a narrative, a dialogue, a drama; it has been successfully acted as a one-act play. Three people are portrayed: a farmer, his wife, and an old incompetent hired hand, shiftless and proud – and the character most fully revealed is the one who never appears.

The poem has endeared itself to readers of every kind, and for many reasons. Some readers have praised it for its authentic power, its conversational beauty, its rich sense of ordinary life. Others have been won by its eloquent descriptions, particularly by such a passage as:

> Part of a moon was falling down the west,
> Dragging the whole sky with it to the hills.
> Its light poured softly in her lap. She saw it
> And spread her apron to it. She put out her hand
> Among the harp-like morning-glory strings,
> Taut with the dew from garden bed to eaves,
> As if she played unheard some tenderness
> That wrought on him beside her in the night.

Perhaps the most famous lines in the poem are those in which husband and wife trade definitions of home. Here the mood changes, and light irony is exchanged for deep pathos. The husband's mocking definition is offered first:

> 'Home is the place where, when you have to go there,
> They have to take you in.'

To which the wife, with a reproving mildness, replies:

> 'I should have called it
> Something you somehow haven't to deserve.'

'The Death of the Hired Man' is one of the most touching human episodes, the more so since it is all so quiet. The story unfolds itself in understones; a poem heard – or overheard – in whispers.

The Death of the Hired Man

Mary sat musing on the lamp-flame at the table
Waiting for Warren. When she heard his step,
She ran on tiptoe down the darkened passage
To meet him in the doorway with the news
And put him on his guard. 'Silas is back.'
She pushed him outward with her through the door
And shut it after her. 'Be kind,' she said.
She took the market things from Warren's arms
And set them on the porch, then drew him down
To sit beside her on the wooden steps.

'When was I ever anything but kind to him?
But I'll not have the fellow back,' he said.

'I told him so last haying, didn't I?
"If he left then," I said, "that ended it."
What good is he? Who else will harbour him
At his age for the little he can do?
What help he is there's no depending on.
Off he goes always when I need him most.
"He thinks he ought to earn a little pay,
Enough at least to buy tobacco with,
So he won't have to beg and be beholden."
"All right," I say, "I can't afford to pay
Any fixed wages, though I wish I could."
"Someone else can." "Then someone else will have to."
I shouldn't mind his bettering himself
If that was what it was. You can be certain,
When he begins like that, there's someone at him
Trying to coax him off with pocket-money, –
In haying time, when any help is scarce.
In winter he comes back to us. I'm done.'

'Sh! not so loud: he'll hear you,' Mary said.

'I want him to: he'll have to soon or late.'

'He's worn out. He's asleep beside the stove.
When I came up from Rowe's I found him here,
Huddled against the barn-door fast asleep,
A miserable sight, and frightening, too –
You needn't smile – I didn't recognize him –
I wasn't looking for him – and he's changed.
Wait till you see.'

        'Where did you say he'd been?'

'He didn't say. I dragged him to the house,
And gave him tea and tried to make him smoke.
I tried to make him talk about his travels.
Nothing would do: he just kept nodding off.'

'What did he say? Did he say anthing?'

'But little.'

       'Anything? Mary, confess
He said he'd come to ditch the meadow for me.'

'Warren!'

      'But did he? I just want to know.'

'Of course he did. What would you have him say?
Surely you wouldn't grudge the poor old man
Some humble way to save his self-respect.
He added, if you really care to know,
He meant to clear the upper pasture, too.
That sounds like something you have heard before?
Warren, I wish you could have heard the way
He jumbled everything. I stopped to look

Two or three times – he made me feel so queer –
To see if he was talking in his sleep.
He ran on Harold Wilson – you remember –
The boy you had in haying four years since.
He's finished school, and teaching in his college.
Silas declares you'll have to get him back.
He says they two will make a team for work:
Between them they will lay this farm as smooth!
The way he mixed that in with other things.
He thinks young Wilson a likely lad, though daft
On education – you know how they fought
All through July under the blazing sun,
Silas up on the cart to build the load,
Harold along beside to pitch it on.'

'Yes, I took care to keep well out of earshot.'

'Well, those days trouble Silas like a dream.
You wouldn't think they would. How some things linger!
Harold's young college boy's assurance piqued him.
After so many years he still keeps finding
Good arguments he sees he might have used.
I sympathize, I know just how it feels
To think of the right thing to say too late.
Harold's associated in his mind with Latin.
He asked me what I thought of Harold's saying
He studied Latin like the violin
Because he liked it – that an argument!
He said he couldn't make the boy believe
He could find water with a hazel prong –
Which showed how much good school had ever done him.
He wanted to go over that. But most of all
He thinks if he could have another chance
To teach him how to build a load of hay –'

'I know, that's Silas' one accomplishment.
He bundles every forkful in its place,
And tags and numbers it for future reference,
So he can find and easily dislodge it
In the unloading. Silas does that well.
He takes it out in bunches like big birds' nests.
You never see him standing on the hay
He's trying to lift, straining to lift himself.'

'He thinks if he could teach him that, he'd be
Some good perhaps to someone in the world.
He hates to see a boy the fool of books.
Poor Silas, so concerned for other folk,
And nothing to look backward to with pride,
And nothing to look forward to with hope,
So now and never any different.'

Part of a moon was falling down the west,

Dragging the whole sky with it to the hills.
Its light poured softly in her lap. She saw it
And spread her apron to it. She put out her hand
Among the harp-like morning-glory strings,
Taut with the dew from garden bed to eaves,
As if she played unheard some tenderness
That wrought on him beside her in the night.
'Warren,' she said, 'he has come home to die:
You needn't be afraid he'll leave you this time.'

'Home,' he mocked gently.

      'Yes, what else but home?
It all depends on what you mean by home.
Of course he's nothing to us, any more
Than was the hound that came a stranger to us
Out of the woods, worn out upon the trail.'

'Home is the place where, when you have to go there,
They have to take you in.'

     'I should have called it
Something you somehow haven't to deserve.'

Warren leaned out and took a step or two,
Picked up a little stick, and brought it back
And broke it in his hand and tossed it by.
'Silas has better claim on us you think
Than on his brother? Thirteen little miles
As the road winds would bring him to his door.
Silas has walked that far no doubt to-day.
Why didn't he go there? His brother's rich,
A somebody – director in the bank.'

'He never told us that'.

     'We know it though.'

'I think his brother ought to help, of course.

I'll see to that if there is need. He ought of right
To take him in, and might be willing to –
He may be better than appearances.
But have some pity on Silas. Do you think
If he had any pride in claiming kin
Or anything he looked for from his brother,
He'd keep so still about him all this time?'

'I wonder what's between them.'

     'I can tell you.
Silas is what he is – we wouldn't mind him –
But just the kind that kinsfolk can't abide.
He never did a thing so very bad.
He don't know why he isn't quite as good
As anybody. Worthless though he is,
He won't be made ashamed to please his brother.'

'*I* can't think Si ever hurt anyone.'

'No, but he hurt my heart the way he lay
And rolled his old head on that sharp-edged chair-back;
He wouldn't let me put him on the lounge.
You must go in and see what you can do.
I made the bed up for him there to-night.
You'll be surprised at him – how much he's broken.
His working days are done; I'm sure of it.'

'I'd not be in a hurry to say that.'

'I haven't been. Go, look, see for yourself.
But, Warren, please remember how it is:
He's come to help you ditch the meadow.
He has a plan. You mustn't laugh at him.
He may not speak of it, and then he may.
I'll sit and see if that small sailing cloud
Will hit or miss the moon.'

              It hit the moon.
Then there were three there, making a dim row,
The moon, the little silver cloud, and she.

Warren returned – too soon, it seemed to her,
Slipped to her side, caught up her hand and waited.

'Warren?' she questioned.

            'Dead', was all he answered.

Reading and talking

Set the scene and then read the rest of the poem as a dialogue. You will need to pay particular attention to punctuation in order to decide who is speaking.

How is the dialogue used to:
- tell us about the following characters?
  – Mary
  – Warren
  – Silas
  – Silas' brother
  – Harold Wilson
- emphasise the difference in attitude between Mary and Warren?
- sustain interest in the character who never actually appears?
- achieve an easy conversational tone?

Writing

After you have talked about the features of blank verse and the way in which it is used in this poem, try writing your own dialogue using this form, e.g. a conversation between:
- Mary and Silas before Warren's return;
- Warren and Silas' brother in which they discuss the death of the hired man.

Drama

Make a tape recording of part of the poem and any of your own writing. Use appropriate sound effects to help to establish atmosphere.

Talking

Now that you have explored the poem through a variety of activities, look back at Louis Untermeyer's commentary.

Do you agree with the powerful claims he makes for the appeal of this poem? How valuable do you find his introduction as a model for writing your own commentaries?

DRAMA

She Stoops to Conquer, Oliver Goldsmith

The most important way in which the playwright can create a character is through dialogue. Whilst it must sound realistic and natural, play dialogue is not the language of real life, in which conversations are often rambling, repetitive and lacking in interest. Play dialogue has to be shaped and ordered in order to heighten dramatic tension and impact.

Certain theatrical devices with regard to speech have also been developed which do not happen in everyday situations. For example, we accept as an audience that it is perfectly natural for a character to speak her thoughts aloud (*soliloquy*) and also to communicate with the audience without the other characters seeming to hear (*aside*).

Another convention is that plays may be written in verse form; in Elizabethan times, all plays were written in verse and more recently, T. S. Eliot, Christopher Fry and Dylan Thomas have revived this genre.

What dialogue can do

Dialogue can:
- express ideas and make characters come alive in the fewest possible words;
- comment upon what is happening as well as furthering the plot;
- remind the audience of what has already happened;
- set up dramatic tension;
- relieve tension, sometimes through humour;
- introduce a character through what is said before the character actually appears;
- *reveal* more about a character, e.g. feelings, opinions, attitudes, manner, social position, accent, intelligence and mood at the moment of speaking;
- *hide* what a character might be thinking or feeling. Sometimes there is a marked difference between a character's words and actions (*dramatic irony*);
- establish relationships between characters.

Let us now look at *She Stoops to Conquer* as an example.

Prior to the point at which we take up the play in Act 3, we have been introduced to Marlow and his friend Hastings. A joke played on the two young gentlemen by Miss Hardcastle's brother has led them to believe that the Hardcastle's country house is an inn and Mr Hardcastle, the innkeeper. Mr Hardcastle is bewildered by Marlow's ill-mannered behaviour, particularly as he had been invited as a possible husband for his daughter.

A further example of irony is the fact that Marlow is normally excrutiatingly shy with ladies of good breeding, as was plain when he was first introduced to Kate Hardcastle whom he believed must be, like himself, a visitor to 'the inn'. When he meets her again, however, mistaking her for the maid, he reveals another side to his character!

[*Enter* MISS HARDCASTLE *and* MAID]

MISS HARD What an unaccountable creature is that brother of mine, to send them to the house as an inn, ha, ha. I don't wonder at his impudence.

MAID But what is more, Madam, the young gentleman as you passed by in your present dress, ask'd me if you were the barmaid? He mistook you for the barmaid, Madam.

MISS HARD Did he? Then as I live I'm resolved to keep up the delusion. Tell me, Pimple, how do you like my present dress? Don't you think I look something like Cherry in the Beaux' Stratagem?

MAID It's the dress, Madam, that every lady wears in the country, but when she visits or receives company.

MISS HARD And are you sure he does not remember my face or person?

MAID Certain of it.

MISS HARD I vow I thought so; for though we spoke for some time together, yet his fears were such, that he never once looked up during the interview. Indeed, if he had, my bonnet would have kept him from seeing me.

MAID But what do you hope from keeping him in his mistake.

MISS HARD In the first place, I shall be *seen*, and that is no small advantage to a girl who brings her face to market. Then I shall perhaps make an acquaintance, and that's no small victory gained over one who never addresses any but the wildest of her sex. But my chief aim is to take my gentleman off his guard, and like an invisible champion of romance examine the giant's force before I offer to combat.

MAID But are you sure you can act your part, and disguise your voice, so that he may mistake that, as he has already mistaken your person?

MISS HARD Never fear me. I think I have got the true bar cant – Did your honour call? – Attend the Lion there. – Pipes and tobacco for the Angel. – The Lamb has been outrageous this half hour.

MAID   It will do, Madam. But he's here. [*Exit* MAID]

[*Enter* MARLOW]

MARL   What a bawling in every part of the house; I have scarce a
moment's repose. If I go to the best room, there I find my host
and his story . If I fly to the gallery, there we have my hostess
with her curtesy down to the ground. I have at last got a
moment to myself, and now for recollection. [*Walks and muses*]

MISS HARD   Did you call, Sir? Did your honour call?

MARL   [*Musing*] As for Miss Hardcastle, she's too grave and
sentimental for me.

MISS HARD   Did your honour call?

[*She still places herself before him, he turning away*]

MARL   No, child. [*Musing*] Besides, from the glimpse I had of her,
I think she squints.

MISS HARD   I'm sure, Sir, I heard the bell ring.

MARL   No, no. [*Musing*] I have pleased my father, however, by
coming down, and I'll to-morrow please myself by returning.
[*Taking out his tablets, and perusing*]

MISS HARD   Perhaps the other gentlemen called, Sir?

MARL   I tell you, no.

MISS HARD   I should be glad to know, Sir. We have such a parcel
of servants.

MARL   No, no, I tell you. [*Looks full in her face*] Yes, child. I think
I did call. I wanted – I wanted – I vow, child, you are vastly
handsome.

MISS HARD   O la, Sir, you 'll make one asham'd.

MARL   Never saw a more sprightly malicious eye. Yes, yes, my
dear, I did call. Have you got any of your – a – what d'ye call it,
in the house?

MISS HARD   No, Sir, we have been out of that these ten days.

MARL   One may call in this house, I find, to very little purpose.
Suppose I should call for a taste, just by way of trial, of the
nectar of your lips; perhaps I might be disappointed in that
too.

MISS HARD   Nectar! nectar! that's a liquor there's no call for in
these parts. French, I suppose. We keep no French wines here,
Sir.

MARL   Of true English growth, I assure you.

MISS HARD   Then it's odd I should not know it. We brew all sorts
of wines in this house, and I have lived here these eighteen
years.

MARL   Eighteen years! Why one would think, child, you kept the
bar before you were born. How old are you?

MISS HARD   O! Sir, I must not tell my age. They say women and
music should never be dated.

MARL   To guess at this distance, you can't be much above forty
[*approaching*]. Yet nearer I don't think so much [*approaching*]. By
coming close to some women, they look younger still; but when
we come very close indeed – [*attempting to kiss her*].

MISS HARD   Pray, Sir, keep your distance. One would think you
wanted to know one's age as they do horses, by mark of mouth.

MARL   I protest, child, you use me extremely ill. If you keep me at this distance, how is it possible you and I can ever be acquainted.

MISS HARD   And who wants to be acquainted with you? I want no such acquaintance, not I. I'm sure you did not treat Miss Hardcastle that was here awhile ago in this obstropalous manner. I'll warrant me, before her you look'd dash'd, and kept bowing to the ground, and talk'd, for all the world, as if you was before a justice of peace.

MARL   [*Aside*] Egad! She has hit it, sure enough. [*To her*] In awe of her, child? Ha! ha! ha! A mere, awkward squinting thing, no, no. I find you don't know me. I laugh'd and rallied her a little; but I was unwilling to be too severe. No, I could not be too severe, *curse me*!

MISS HARD   O! then, Sir, you are a favourite, I find, among the ladies?

MARL   Yes, my dear, a great favourite. And yet, hang me, I don't see what they find in me to follow. At the Ladies' Club in town I'm called their agreeable Rattle. Rattle, child, is not my real name, but one I'm known by. My name is Solomons. Mr. Solomons, my dear, at your service. [*Offering to salute her*]

MISS HARD   Hold, Sir; you are introducing me to your club, not to yourself. And you're so great a favourite there, you say?

MARL   Yes, my dear. There's Mrs. Mantrap, Lady Betty Blackleg, the Countess of Sligo, Mrs. Langhorns, old Miss Biddy Buckskin, and your humble servant, keep up the spirit of the place.

MISS HARD   Then it's a very merry place, I suppose?

MARL   Yes, as merry as cards, suppers. wine, and old women can make us.

MISS HARD   And their agreeable Rattle, ha! ha! ha!

MARL   [*Aside*] Egad! I don't quite like this chit. She seems knowing, methinks. You laugh, child!

MISS HARD   I can't but laugh to think what time they all have for minding their work or their family.

MARL   [*Aside*] All's well; she don't laugh at me. [*To her*] Do you ever work, child?

MISS HARD   Ay, sure. There's not a screen or a quilt in the whole house but what can bear witness to that.

MARL   Odso! Then you must shew me your embroidery. I embroider and draw patterns myself a little. If you want a judge of your work you must apply to me. [*Seizing her hand*]

MISS HARD   Ay, but the colours do not look well by candle light. You shall see all in the morning. [*Struggling*]

MARL   And why not now, my angel? Such beauty fires beyond the power of resistance. – Pshaw! the father here! My old luck: I never nick'd seven that I did not throw ames ace three times following. [*Exit* MARLOW]

[*Enter* HARDCASTLE, *who stands in surprise.*]

HARD   So, Madam! So I find *this* is your *modest* lover. This is your humble admirer that kept his eyes fixed on the ground, and only ador'd at humble distance. Kate, Kate, art thou not asham'd to deceive your father so.

MISS HARD   Never trust me, dear Papa, but he's still the modest man I first took him for, you'll be convinced of it as well as I.

HARD   By the hand of my body, I believe his impudence is infectious! Didn't I see him seize your hand? Didn't I see him hawl you about like a milk maid? and now you talk of his respect and his modesty, forsooth!

MISS HARD   But if I shortly convince you of his modesty, that he has only the faults that will pass off with time; and the virtues that will improve with age, I hope you'll forgive him.

HARD   The girl would actually make one run mad! I tell you I'll not be convinced. I am convinced. He has scarce been three hours in the house, and he has already encroached on all my prerogatives. You may like his impudence, and call it modesty. But my son-in-law, Madam, must have very different qualifications.

Reading   Read the extract in pairs. Note the point at which Kate Hardcastle takes on the role of barmaid and changes her accent in order to make the character convincing.

Writing   Think about theatrical conventions and the purpose of dialogue. By close reference to the text, give examples of the playwright's use of both in this extract.

Write down the *unexpressed* thoughts of either Kate Hardcastle or Marlow during their encounter in this scene.

Marlow is caught in the act by Kate Hardcastle's father

DRAMA

Hobson's Choice, Harold Brighouse

We'll now look at the scene in this play in which Maggie Hobson proposes to Will Mossop.

WILLIE   Yes, Miss Maggie?

MAGGIE   Come up, and put the trap down; I want to talk to you. [*He comes, reluctantly.*]

WILLIE   We're very busy in the cellar. [MAGGIE *points to trap. He closes it.*]

MAGGIE   Show me your hands, Willie.

WILLIE   They're dirty. [*He holds them out hesitatingly.*]

MAGGIE   Yes, they're dirty, but they're clever. They can shape the leather like no other man's that ever came into the shop. Who taught you, Willie? [*She retains his hands.*]

WILLIE   Why, Miss Maggie, I learnt my trade here.

MAGGIE   Hobson's never taught you to make boots the way you do.

WILLIE   I've had no other teacher.

MAGGIE   [*dropping his hands*] And needed none. You're a natural born genius at making boots. It's a pity you're a natural fool at all else.

WILLIE   I'm not much good at owt but leather, and that's a fact.

MAGGIE   When are you going to leave Hobson's?

WILLIE   Leave Hobson's? I – I thought I gave satisfaction.

MAGGIE   Don't you want to leave?

WILLIE   Not me. I've been at Hobson's all my life, and I'm not leaving till I'm made.

MAGGIE   I said you were a fool.

WILLIE   Then I'm a loyal fool.

MAGGIE   Don't you want to get on, Will Mossop? You heard what Mrs Hepworth said. You know the wages you get and you know the wages a bootmaker like you could get in one of the big shops in Manchester.

WILLIE   Nay, I'd be feared to go in them fine places.

MAGGIE   What keeps you here? Is it the – the people?

WILLIE   I dunno what it is. I'm used to being here.

MAGGIE   Do you know what keeps this business on its legs? Two things: one's the good boots you make that sell themselves, the other's the bad boots other people make and I sell. We're a pair, Will Mossop.

WILLIE   You're a wonder in the shop, Miss Maggie.

MAGGIE   And you're a marvel in the workshop. Well?

WILLIE   Well, what?

MAGGIE   It seems to me to point one way.

WILLIE   What way is that?

MAGGIE   You're leaving me to do the work, my lad.

WILLIE   I'll be getting back to my stool, Miss Maggie.

[*Moves to trap.*]

MAGGIE   [*stopping him*] You'll go back when I've done with you. I've watched you for a long time and everything I've seen, I've liked. I think you'll do for me.

WILLIE   What way, Miss Maggie?

MAGGIE   Will Mossop, you're my man. Six months I've counted on you and it's got to come out some time.

WILLIE   But I never –

MAGGIE   I know you never, or it 'ud not be left to me to do the job like this.

WILLIE   I'll – I'll sit down. [*He sits in arm-chair, mopping his brow.*] I'm feeling queer-like. What dost want me for?

MAGGIE   To invest in. You're a business idea in the shape of a man.

WILLIE   I've got no head for business at all.

MAGGIE   But I have. My brain and your hands 'ull make a working partnership.

WILLIE   [*getting up, relieved*] Partnership! Oh, that's a different thing. I thought you were axing me to wed you.

MAGGIE   I am.

WILLIE   Well, by gum! And you the master's daughter.

MAGGIE   Maybe that's why, Will Mossop. Maybe I've had enough of father, and you're as different from him as any man I know.

WILLIE   It's a bit awkward-like.

MAGGIE   And you don't help me any, lad. What's awkward about it?

WILLIE   You talking to me like this.

MAGGIE   I'll tell you something, Will. It's a poor sort of woman who'll stay lazy when she sees her best chance slipping from her. A Salford life's too near the bone to lose things through fear of speaking out.

WILLIE   I'm your best chance?

MAGGIE   You are that, Will.

WILLIE   Well, by gum! I never thought of this.

MAGGIE   Think of it now.

WILLIE   I am doing. Only the blow's a bit too sudden to think very clear. I've a great respect for you, Miss Maggie. You're a shapely body, and you're a masterpiece at selling in the shop, but when it comes to marrying, I'm bound to tell you that I'm none in love with you.

MAGGIE   Wait till you're asked. I want your hand in mine and your word for it that you'll go through life with me for the best we can get out of it.

WILLIE   We'd not get much without there's love between us, lass.

MAGGIE   I've got the love all right.

WILLIE   Well, I've not, and that's honest.

MAGGIE   We'll get along without.

WILLIE   You're desperate set on this. It's a puzzle to me all ways. What'ud your father say?

MAGGIE   He'll say a lot, and he can say it. It'll make no difference to me.

WILLIE   Much better not upset him. It's not worth while.

MAGGIE   I'm judge of that. You're going to wed me, Will.

WILLIE   Oh, nay, I'm not. Really I can't do that, Maggie. I can see that I'm disturbing your arrangements like, but I'll be obliged if you'll put this notion from you.

MAGGIE   When I make arrangements, my lad, they're not made for upsetting.

WILLIE   What makes it so desperate awkward is that I'm tokened.

MAGGIE   You're what?

WILLIE   I'm tokened to Ada Figgins.

MAGGIE   Then you'll get loose and quick. Who's Ada Figgins? Do I know her?

WILLIE   I'm the lodger at her mother's.

MAGGIE   The scheming hussy. It's not that sandy girl who brings your dinner?

WILLIE   She's golden-haired is Ada. Aye, she'll be here soon.

MAGGIE   And so shall I. I'll talk to Ada. I've seen her and I know the breed. Ada's the helpless sort.

WILLIE   She needs protecting.

MAGGIE   That's how she got you, was it? Yes, I can see her clinging round your neck, until you fancied you were strong. But I'll tell you this, my lad, it's a desperate poor kind of a woman that'll look for protection to the likes of you.

WILLIE   Ada does.

MAGGIE   And that gives me the weight of her. She's born to meekness, Ada is. You wed her, and you'll be an eighteen shilling a week bootmaker all the days of your life. You'll be a slave, and a contented slave.

WILLIE   I'm not ambitious that I know of.

MAGGIE   No. But you're going to be. I'll see to that. I've got my work cut out, but there's the makings of a man about you.

WILLIE   I wish you'd leave me alone.

MAGGIE   So does the fly when the spider catches him. You're my man, Willie Mossop.

Reading

Work in pairs.

In your reading, try to achieve both the Lancashire dialect and the outspoken, direct tone which typifies the speech of both these characters.

Talking

- Discuss the economy of the dialogue and the 'shaping' of the scene.
- To what extent does the dialogue have the sound of normal speech?
- How far does the dialogue help the actors to create characterisation?
- What are the main purposes of this dialogue?
- Jot down quotations which seem to point to what the next act will be about.
- How does the playwright make use of the element of surprise in this scene?

DRAMA

The Birthday Party, Harold Pinter

This scene, from Act 1, is the final example of dialogue in drama form.

[The living-room of a house in a seaside town. A door leading to the hall down left. Back door and small window up left. Kitchen hatch, centre back. Kitchen door up right. Table and chairs, centre.

PETEY *enters from the door on the left with a paper and sits at the table. He begins to read.* MEG's *voice comes through the kitchen hatch.]*

MEG   Is that you, Petey?
     [Pause.]
     Petey, is that you?
     [Pause.]
     Petey?

PETEY   What?

MEG   Is that you?

PETEY   Yes, it's me.

MEG   What? *[Her face appears at the hatch.]* Are you back?

PETEY   Yes.

MEG   I've got your cornflakes ready. *[She disappears and re-appears.]* Here's your cornflakes.
     [He rises and takes the plate from her, sits at the table, props up the paper and begins to eat. MEG *enters by the kitchen door.]*
     Are they nice?

PETEY   Very nice.

MEG   I thought they'd be nice. *[She sits at the table.]* You got your paper?

PETEY   Yes.

MEG   Is it good?

PETEY   Not bad.

MEG   What does it say?

PETEY   Nothing much.

MEG   You read me out some nice bits yesterday.

PETEY   Yes, well, I haven't finished this one yet.

MEG   Will you tell me when you come to something good?

PETEY   Yes.
     [Pause.]

MEG   Have you been working hard this morning?

PETEY   No. Just stacked a few of the old chairs. Cleaned up a bit.

MEG   Is it nice out?

PETEY   Very nice.
     [Pause.]

MEG   Is Stanley up yet?

PETEY   I don't know. Is he?

MEG   I don't know. I haven't seen him down yet.

PETEY   Well then, he can't be up.

MEG   Haven't you seen him down?

PETEY I've only just come in.

MEG He must be still asleep. [*She looks round the room, stands, goes to the sideboard and takes a pair of socks from a drawer, collects wool and a needle and goes back to the table.*] What time did you go out this morning, Petey?

PETEY Same time as usual.

MEG Was it dark?

PETEY No, it was light.

MEG [*beginning to darn.*]: But sometimes you go out in the morning and it's dark.

PETEY That's in the winter.

MEG Oh, in winter.

PETEY Yes, it gets light later in winter.

MEG Oh.

[*Pause.*]

What are you reading?

PETEY Someone's just had a baby.

MEG Oh, they haven't! Who?

PETEY Some girl.

MEG Who, Petey, who?

PETEY I don't think you'd know her.

MEG What's her name?

PETEY Lady Mary Splatt.

MEG I don't know her.

PETEY No.

MEG What is it?

PETEY [*studying the paper.*] Er – a girl.

MEG Not a boy?

PETEY No.

MEG Oh, what a shame. I'd be sorry. I'd much rather have a little boy.

PETEY A little girl's all right.

MEG I'd much rather have a little boy.

[*Pause.*]

PETEY I've finished my cornflakes.

MEG Were they nice?

PETEY Very nice.

MEG I've got something else for you.

PETEY Good.

Reading

Practise reading this dialogue aloud in pairs. Decide what effect you want to have on your 'audience'. For example, is it your aim to amuse, to make uneasy, to anger or to surprise, etc? Share your interpretations and comment on any differences.

Talking and writing

■ How does Pinter achieve the effect of characters talking and listening to themselves? Is it 'real life' conversation?

■ What use is made of silence in this extract?

■ Do you think his characters are saying all that is in their minds?

■ Continue the dialogue. It is not as easy as you think!

■ Compare and contrast these three scenes, paying particular

attention to characterisation, language and humour.
■ Which of the extracts has interested you enough to make you
want to read the whole play?

Drama

Any of the extracts might be particularly useful for drama students
preparing for a practical drama examination.

Improvisation pieces which take up the main themes could
precede or follow the scripts.

6

Into a script

DRAMA

The Crucible, Arthur Miller

Talk, writing, background research and especially improvisation and role play will have helped to deepen your understanding of the ideas and underlying themes in chosen play texts. You may also have been fortunate enough to see a performance of the play on stage or television.

During your course and particularly for revision, you will be required to answer questions such as might be set in an English or Drama written examination. To answer successfully, you must be able to visualise characters moving, speaking and relating to each other in their setting; to get inside a script, make it live inside your head.

We have chosen two extracts from *The Crucible* by Arthur Miller. The play, based on historical fact, is set in 1692 in Salem, Massachusetts and tells the story of the effects on a strictly Puritan community of rumours that witchcraft and black magic were being widely practised. Even the most unlikely and much respected citizens were caught up in the witch hunt. False accusations borne out of suspicion and envy caused bitter rifts between neighbours, friends, children, wives and their husbands. Many people were hanged.

Some of you may already be studying this play; for others the extracts will appear as 'unseen texts'. Whichever category you fall into, all of you will have a knowledge of how plays work and that they are concerned with situation, characters, dialogue, setting, dramatic effects and stage directions.

One way of revising plays is to focus on the relationship between two main characters and to trace its development. In this play, the relationship between John and Elizabeth Proctor is crucial to our understanding of the whole play.

The first extract is from Act 2.

[*The common room of Proctor's house, eight days later.*

At the right is a door opening on the fields outside. A fireplace is at the left, and behind it a stairway leading upstairs. It is the low, dark, and rather long living-room of the time. As the curtain rises, the room is empty. From above, ELIZABETH *is heard softly singing to the children. Presently the door opens and* JOHN PROCTOR *enters, carrying his gun. He glances about the room as he comes toward the fireplace, then halts for an instant as he hears her singing. He continues on to the fireplace, leans the gun against the wall as he swings a pot out of the fire and smells it. Then he lifts out the ladle and tastes. He is not quite pleased. He reaches to a cupboard, takes a pinch of salt, and drops it into the pot. As he is tasting again, her footsteps are heard on the stair. He swings the pot into the fireplace and goes to a basin and washes his hands and face.* ELIZABETH *enters.*]

ELIZABETH   What keeps you so late? It's almost dark.

PROCTOR   I were planting far out to the forest edge.

ELIZABETH   Oh, you're done then.

PROCTOR   Aye, the farm is seeded. The boys asleep?

ELIZABETH   They will be soon. [*And she goes to the fireplace, proceeds to ladle up stew in a dish.*]

PROCTOR   Pray now for a fair summer.

ELIZABETH   Aye.

PROCTOR   Are you well today?

ELIZABETH   I am. [*She brings the plate to the table, and, indicating the food*] It is a rabbit.

PROCTOR   [*going to the table*] Oh, is it! In Jonathan's trap?

ELIZABETH   No, she walked into the house this afternoon; I found her sittin' in the corner like she come to visit.

PROCTOR   Oh, that's a good sign walkin' in.

ELIZABETH   Pray God. It hurt my heart to strip her, poor rabbit. [*She sits and watches him taste it.*]

PROCTOR   It's well seasoned.

ELIZABETH   [*blushing with pleasure*] I took great care. She's tender?

PROCTOR   Aye. [*He eats. She watches him.*] I think we'll see green fields soon. It's warm as blood beneath the clods.

ELIZABETH   That's well.
[*Proctor eats, then looks up.*]

PROCTOR   If the crop is good I'll buy George Jacob's heifer. How would that please you?

ELIZABETH   Aye, it would.

PROCTOR   [*with a grin*] I mean to please you, Elizabeth.

ELIZABETH   [*it is hard to say*] I know it, John.
[*He gets up, goes to her, kisses her. She receives it. With a certain disappointment, he returns to the table.*]

PROCTOR   [*as gently as he can*] Cider?

ELIZABETH   [*with a sense of reprimanding herself for having forgot*] Aye! [*She gets up and goes and pours a glass for him. He now arches his back.*]

PROCTOR   This farm's a continent when you go foot by foot droppin' seeds in it.

ELIZABETH   [*coming with the cider*] It must be.

PROCTOR   [*drinks a long draught, then, putting the glass down*] You ought to bring some flowers in the house.

ELIZABETH   Oh, I forgot! I will tomorrow.

PROCTOR   It's winter in here yet. On Sunday let you come with me, and we'll walk the farm together; I never see such a load of flowers on the earth. [*With good feeling he goes and looks up at the sky through the open doorway.*] Lilacs have a purple smell. Lilac is the smell of nightfall, I think. Massachusetts is a beauty in the spring!

ELIZABETH   Aye, it is.

[*There is a pause. She is watching him from the table as he stands there absorbing the night. It is as though she would speak but cannot. Instead, now, she takes up his plate and glass and fork and goes with them to the basin. Her back is turned to him. He turns to her and watches her. A sense of their separation rises.*]

PROCTOR   I think you're sad again. Are you?

ELIZABETH   [*she doesn't want friction, and yet she must*] You come so late I thought you'd gone to Salem this afternoon.

PROCTOR   Why? I have no business in Salem.

ELIZABETH   You did speak of going, earlier this week.

PROCTOR   [*he knows what she means*] I thought better of it since.

ELIZABETH   Mary Warren's there today.

PROCTOR   Why'd you let her? You heard me forbid her go to Salem any more!

ELIZABETH   I couldn't stop her.

PROCTOR   [*holding back a full condemnation of her*] It is a fault, it is a fault, Elizabeth – you're the mistress here, not Mary Warren.

ELIZABETH   She frightened all my strength away.

PROCTOR   How may that mouse frighten you, Elizabeth? You –

ELIZABETH   It is a mouse no more. I forbid her go, and she raises up her chin like the daughter of a prince and says to me, 'I must go to Salem, Goody Proctor; I am an official of the court!'

PROCTOR   Court! What court?

ELIZABETH   Aye, it is a proper court they have now. They've sent four judges out of Boston, she says, weighty magistrates of the General Court, and at the head sits the Deputy Governor of the Province.

PROCTOR   [*astonished*] Why, she's mad.

ELIZABETH   I would to God she were. There be fourteen people in the jail now, she says.

[PROCTOR *simply looks at her, unable to grasp it.*]

And they'll be tried, and the court have power to hang them too, she says.

PROCTOR   [*scoffing, but without conviction*] Ah, they'd never hang –

ELIZABETH   The Deputy Governor promise hangin' if they'll not confess, John. The town's gone wild, I think. She speak of Abigail, and I thought she were a saint, to hear her. Abigail brings the other girls into the court, and where she walks the crowd will part like the sea for Israel. And folks are brought before them, and if they scream and howl and fall to the floor – the person's clapped in the jail for bewitchin' them.

PROCTOR   [*wide-eyed*] Oh, it is a black mischief.

ELIZABETH   I think you must go to Salem, John.

[*He turns to her.*]

I think so. You must tell them it is a fraud.

PROCTOR   [*thinking beyond this*] Aye, it is, it is surely.

ELIZABETH   Let you go to Ezekiel Cheever – he knows you well. And tell him what she said to you last week in her uncle's house. She said it had naught to do with witchcraft, did she not?

PROCTOR   [*in thought*] Aye, she did, she did.

[*Now, a pause.*]

ELIZABETH [*quietly, fearing to anger him by prodding*] God forbid you keep that from the court, John. I think they must be told.

PROCTOR [*quietly, struggling with his thought*] Aye, they must, they must. It is a wonder they do believe her.

ELIZABETH I would go to Salem now, John – let you go tonight.

PROCTOR I'll think on it.

ELIZABETH [*with her courage now*] You cannot keep it, John.

PROCTOR [*angering*] I know I cannot keep it. I say I will think on it!

ELIZABETH [*hurt, and very coldly*] Good, then, let you think on it.
[*She stands and starts to walk out of the room.*]

PROCTOR I am only wondering how I may prove what she told me, Elizabeth. If the girl's a saint now, I think it is not easy to prove she's fraud, and the town gone so silly. She told it to me in a room alone – I have no proof for it.

ELIZABETH You were alone with her?

PROCTOR [*stubbornly*] For a moment alone, aye.

ELIZABETH Why, then, it is not as you told me.

PROCTOR [*his anger rising*] For a moment, I say. The others come in soon after.

ELIZABETH [*quietly – she has suddenly lost all faith in him*] Do as you wish, then. [*She starts to turn.*]

PROCTOR Woman.
[*She turns to him.*]
I'll not have your suspicion any more.

ELIZABETH [*a little loftily*] I have no –

PROCTOR I'll not have it!

ELIZABETH Then let you not earn it.

PROCTOR [*with a violent undertone*] You doubt me yet?

ELIZABETH [*with a smile, to keep her dignity*] John, if it were not Abigail that you must go to hurt, would you falter now? I think not.

PROCTOR Now look you –

ELIZABETH I see what I see, John.

PROCTOR [*with solemn warning*] You will not judge me more, Elizabeth. I have good reason to think before I charge fraud on Abigail, and I will think on it. Let you look to your own improvement before you go to judge your husband any more. I have forgot Abigail, and –

ELIZABETH And I.

PROCTOR Spare me! You forget nothin' and forgive nothin'. Learn charity, woman. I have gone tiptoe in this house all seven month since she is gone. I have not moved from there to there without I think to please you, and still an everlasting funeral marches round your heart. I cannot speak but I am doubted, every moment judged for lies, as though I come into a court when I come into this house!

ELIZABETH John, you are not open with me. You saw her with a crowd, you said. Now you –

PROCTOR I'll plead my honesty no more, Elizabeth.

ELIZABETH [*now she would justify herself*]: John, I am only –

PROCTOR   No more! I should have roared you down when first
you told me your suspicion. But I wilted, and, like a Christian,
I confessed. Confessed! Some dream I had must have mistaken
you for God that day. But you're not, you're not, and let you
remember it! Let you look sometimes for the goodness in me,
and judge me not.

ELIZABETH   I do not judge you. The magistrate sits in your heart
that judges you. I never thought you but a good man, John –
[*with a smile*] – only somewhat bewildered.

PROCTOR   [*laughing bitterly*] Oh, Elizabeth, your justice would
freeze beer! [*He turns suddenly toward a sound outside. He starts for
the door as* MARY WARREN *enters. As soon as he sees her, he goes directly
to her and grabs her by her cloak, furious.*] How do you go to Salem
when I forbid it? Do you mock me? [*Shaking her.*] I'll whip you
if you dare leave this house again!
[*Strangely, she doesn't resist him, but hangs limply by his grip.*]

The second extract is from Act 4.

DANFORTH   [*going to her*] Goody Proctor, you are not summoned
here for disputation. Be there no wifely tenderness within you?
He will die with the sunrise. Your husband. Do you
understand it? [*She only looks at him.*] What say you? Will you
contend with him? [*She is silent.*] Are you stone? I tell you true,
woman, had I no other proof of your unnatural life, your dry
eyes now would be sufficient evidence that you delivered up
your soul to Hell! A very ape would weep at such calamity!
Have the devil dried up any tear of pity in you? [*She is silent.*]
Take her out. It profit nothing she should speak to him!

ELIZABETH   [*quietly*] Let me speak with him, Excellency.

PARRIS   [*with hope*] You'll strive with him?
[*She hesitates.*]

DANFORTH   Will you plead for his confession or will you not?

ELIZABETH   I promise nothing. Let me speak with him.
[*A sound – the sibilance of dragging feet on stone. They turn. A pause.*
HERRICK *enters with* JOHN PROCTOR. *His wrists are chained. He is
another man, bearded, filthy, his eyes misty as though webs had overgrown
them. He halts inside the doorway, his eye caught by the sight of*
ELIZABETH. *The emotion flowing between them prevents anyone from
speaking for an instant. Now* HALE, *visibly affected, goes to* DANFORTH
and speaks quietly.]

HALE   Pray, leave them, Excellency.

DANFORTH   [*pressing* HALE *impatiently aside*] Mr Proctor, you have
been notified, have you not?
[PROCTOR *is silent, staring at* ELIZABETH.]
I see light in the sky, Mister; let you counsel with your wife,
and may God help you turn your back on Hell.
[PROCTOR *is silent, staring at* ELIZABETH.]

HALE   [*quietly*] Excellency, let –
[DANFORTH *brushes past* HALE *and walks out.* HALE *follows.*
CHEEVER *stands and follows,* HATHORNE *behind.* HERRICK *goes.*

PARRIS, *from a safe distance, offers:*]

PARRIS If you desire a cup of cider, Mr Proctor, I am sure I –
[PROCTOR *turns an icy stare at him, and he breaks off.*
PARRIS *raises his palms toward* PROCTOR.]
God lead you now. [PARRIS *goes out.*]
[*Alone,* PROCTOR *walks to her, halts. It is as though they stood in a spinning world. It is beyond sorrow, above it. He reaches out his hand as though toward an embodiment not quite real, and as he touches her, a strange soft sound, half laughter, half amazement, comes from his throat. He pats her hand. She covers his hand with hers. And then, weak, he sits. Then she sits, facing him.*]

PROCTOR The child?

ELIZABETH It grows.

PROCTOR There is no word of the boys?

ELIZABETH They're well. Rebecca's Samuel keeps them.

PROCTOR You have not seen them?

ELIZABETH I have not. [*She catches a weakening in herself and downs it.*]

PROCTOR You are a – marvel, Elizabeth.

ELIZABETH You – have been tortured?

PROCTOR Aye.
[*Pause. She will not let herself be drowned in the sea that threatens her.*]
They come for my life now.

ELIZABETH I know it.
[*Pause*]

PROCTOR None – have yet confessed?

ELIZABETH There be many confessed.

PROCTOR Who are they?

ELIZABETH There be a hundred or more, they say. Goody Ballard is one; Isaiah Goodkind is one. There be many.

PROCTOR Rebecca?

ELIZABETH Not Rebecca. She is one foot in Heaven now; naught may hurt her more.

PROCTOR And Giles?

ELIZABETH You have not heard of it?

PROCTOR I hear nothin', where I am kept.

ELIZABETH Giles is dead.
[*He looks at her incredulously.*]

PROCTOR When were he hanged?

ELIZABETH [*quietly, factually*] He were not hanged. He would not answer aye or nay to his indictment; for if he denied the charge they'd hang him surely, and auction out his property. So he stand mute, and died Christian under the law. And so his sons will have his farm. It is the law, for he could not be condemned a wizard without he answer the indictment, aye or nay.

PROCTOR Then how does he die?

ELIZABETH [*gently*] They press him, John.

PROCTOR Press?

ELIZABETH Great stones they lay upon his chest until he plead aye or nay. [*With a tender smile for the old man*] They say he give them but two words. 'More weight,' he says. And died.

PROCTOR [*numbed – a thread to weave into his agony*] 'More weight.'

ELIZABETH   Aye. It were a fearsome man, Giles Corey.
     [*Pause.*]
PROCTOR   [*with great force of will, but not quite looking at her*] I have
     been thinking I would confess to them, Elizabeth. [*She shows
     nothing.*] What say you? If I give them that?
ELIZABETH   I cannot judge you, John.
     [*Pause.*]
PROCTOR   [*simply – a pure question*] What would you have me do?
ELIZABETH   As you will, I would have it. [*Slight pause*] I want you
     living, John. That's sure.
PROCTOR   [*pauses, then with a flailing of hope*] Giles' wife? Have she
     confessed?
ELIZABETH   She will not.
     [*Pause.*]
PROCTOR   It is a pretence, Elizabeth.
ELIZABETH   What is?
PROCTOR   I cannot mount the gibbet like a saint. It is a fraud. I
     am not that man. [*She is silent.*] My honesty is broke, Elizabeth;
     I am no good man. Nothing's spoiled by giving them this lie
     that were not rotten long before.
ELIZABETH   And yet you've not confessed till now. That speak
     goodness in you.
PROCTOR   Spite only keeps me silent. It is hard to give a lie to
     dogs. [*Pause, for the first time he turns directly to her.*] I would have
     your forgiveness, Elizabeth.
ELIZABETH   It is not for me to give, John, I am –
PROCTOR   I'd have you see some honesty in it. Let them that
     never lied die now to keep their souls. It is pretence for me, a
     vanity that will not blind God nor keep my children out of the
     wind. [*Pause.*] What say you?
ELIZABETH   [*upon a heaving sob that always threatens*] John, it come
     to naught that I should forgive you, if you'll not forgive
     yourself.
     [*Now he turns away a little, in great agony.*]
     It is not my soul, John, it is yours.
     [*He stands, as though in physical pain, slowly rising to his feet with a
     great immortal longing to find his answer. It is difficult to say, and she is
     on the verge of tears.*]
     Only be sure of this, for I know it now: Whatever you will do, it
     is a good man does it.
     [*He turns his doubting, searching gaze upon her.*]
     I have read my heart this three month, John. [*Pause.*] I have
     sins of my own to count. It needs a cold wife to prompt lechery.
PROCTOR   [*in great pain*] Enough, enough –
ELIZABETH   [*now pouring out her heart*]: Better you should know me!
PROCTOR   I will not hear it! I know you!
ELIZABETH   You take my sins upon you, John –
PROCTOR   [*in agony*] No, I take my own, my own!
ELIZABETH   John, I counted myself so plain, so poorly made, no
     honest love could come to me! Suspicion kissed you when I did;
     I never knew how I should say my love. It were a cold house I
     kept! [*In fight, she swerves, as* HATHORNE *enters.*]

HATHORNE   What say you, Proctor? The sun is soon up.
[PROCTOR, *his chest heaving, stares, turns to* ELIZABETH.
She comes to him as though to plead, her voice quaking.]
ELIZABETH   Do what you will. But let none be your judge. There
be no higher judge under Heaven than Proctor is! Forgive me,
forgive me, John – I never knew such goodness in the world!
[*She covers her face, weeping.*]

Reading

Working in pairs, read both extracts and explore the dialogues in depth. Discuss what the characters would have said if they had expressed all that was going on in their minds.

Re-read the dialogues in groups of four. Two of you play the characters themselves; two of you play the characters who are going to speak what John and Elizabeth are *thinking* during natural or pre-arranged pauses in the action.

Writing

You are revising these two scenes. Make *notes* for each scene under the following headings.
■ Situation.
■ Character Clues: from stage directions, dialogue, movement, relationship.
■ Mood and Atmosphere: remember to refer to *subtext* (i.e. what is *not* being said).
■ Dramatic Effects: e.g. use of pause, building up tension, climax.

Look at both sets of notes. Those of you who know the play should be able to recall what events have occurred between Act 2 and Act 4. Write a brief synopsis.

If you have not yet read the whole play, it is likely that you will still be able to make general assumptions from the clues given in both extracts. Jot down major changes or developments that have taken place in setting, situation, relationship between characters, mood and atmosphere.

Attempt to answer some of the following questions. It might be a good idea to set your own time limit. Setting *your* own questions and making 'note answers' on selected extracts is a valuable way of revising.

■ What advice would you give to the actress playing Elizabeth Proctor which would help her to bring out the change in her attitude in these two scenes? Refer closely to the text to justify your answer.
■ What advice would you give to the actor playing John Proctor which would help him to bring out the change in his attitude in these two scenes? Refer closely to the text to justify your answer.
■ Draw the set for the beginning of Act 2 which would establish the *place, period* and *atmosphere*. With reference to the text write a brief description justifying your design.
■ You have been chosen to play the part of either John or Elizabeth Proctor. By referring closely to the two scenes, (a) describe your character and (b) outline how, through your

movement and *delivery of lines* you would communicate this character to an audience.

VERSE

Outside the Window, Thomas Hardy

With the decline of the long, narrative poem, a new poetic genre emerged which the poet Vernon Scannell calls the 'narrative lyric'. Poems written in this form resemble ballads in that they focus on a single, dramatic incident but are much shorter and not confined to one set metrical and rhyming pattern.

Many of the short poems of Thomas Hardy (1840–1928) are examples of this form.

Outside the Window

'My stick!' he says, and turns in the lane
To the house just left, whence a vixen voice
Comes out with the firelight through the pane,
And he sees within that the girl of his choice
Stands rating her mother with eyes aglare
For something said while he was there.

'At last I behold her soul undraped!'
Thinks the man who had loved her more than himself;
'My God! – tis but narrowly I have escaped. –
My precious porcelain proves it delf.'
His face has reddened like one ashamed,
And he steals off, leaving his stick unclaimed.

Reading

Read the poem several times.

In his poem, Hardy has managed to present his reader with a whole story on which the imagination can work. It has all the elements essential to drama. Contrast of mood and atmosphere, tension, conflict and irony are subtly hinted at in only twelve lines of verse.

Talking and writing

Tell the story of the poem to another person.

What ideas emerge from this short poem which could form the basis of a one-scene play script? Write a synopsis.

Before writing the first draft of your script you will need to think about the following.

■ What the mother might have said that angered and embarrassed her daughter but went unnoticed by her young man.

- How the 'rating' began; how the quarrel developed and whether any words were *actually* overheard by the young man as he returned to collect his stick.
- How to bring out the satire and humour in the situation through the contrast between the young woman's behaviour whilst her young man is present and her 'vixen'-like attitude towards her mother after he has left.
- Developing the three characters referred to in the poem by writing profiles, giving details of age, physical appearance, background and temperament.
- The behaviour and manners of the period, particularly with regard to courtship and social position.
- Setting the scene by drawing on your knowledge of the Victorian period to establish furniture, furnishings, props and costume.

Drama

Working in small groups, improvise the scene. This will help you to find a shape and appropriate dialogue for your script.

Elect one person from the group to act as observer/recorder. His/her task will be to comment on:
- the development of the story and character;
- the appropriateness of language, jotting down any key phrases which should be included in the written script;
- how effectively the group has managed to capture the movement, mood, atmosphere and contrast in the situation;
- the overall shape of the drama paying particular attention to a suitable ending.

Script writing

Set the scene. Give clear instructions to the producer and the actors. Remember to say your dialogue aloud as you write it.

Share your work; redraft the parts which are least effective and present a final draft for a drama group to work on.

Talking

Discuss what you have learned about human nature in this situation from your study of this poem and from your drama.

Can you think of any present-day situations from your own experience, in which people hide their feelings until they think it is appropriate to reveal them?

Drama

Explore your ideas through improvisation and script writing. Consider the possibility of using them in an anthology programme.

Satires of circumstance
This title was chosen by Thomas Hardy for his collection of short poems of which *Outside the Window* is one example.

You might be interested in compiling your own anthology programme of poetry, prose and drama based on the ideas in some of the other poems in the collection. Two more of Thomas Hardy's poems are included here for your consideration in planning your own work.

At Tea

The kettle descants in a cosy drone,
And the young wife looks in her husband's face,
And then at her guest's, and shows in her own
Her sense that she fills an envied place;
And the visiting lady is all abloom,
And says there was never so sweet a room.

And the happy young housewife does not know
That the woman beside her was first his choice,
Till the fates ordained it could not be so . . . .
Betraying nothing in look or voice
The guest sits smiling and sips her tea,
And he throws her a stray glance yearningly.

In Church

'And now to God the Father,' he ends,
And his voice thrills up to the topmost tiles:
Each listener chokes as he bows and bends,
And emotion pervades the crowded aisles.
Then the preacher glides to the vestry-door,
And shuts it, and thinks he is seen no more.

The door swings softly ajar meanwhile,
And a pupil of his in the Bible class,
Who adores him as one without gloss or guile,
Sees her idol stand with a satisfied smile
And re-enact at the vestry-glass
Each pulpit gesture in deft dumb-show
That had moved the congregation so.

STORY

The Stone, Geraldine O'Donnell

Guidelines to script writers

Selection of material
We have found that short stories are ideal for the purpose of
dramatisation. For a start, choose one which:

■ has a strong story line and which concentrates on a single
  episode;
■ contains a few, well-drawn characters whose relationships you
  clearly understand;
■ already contains some dialogue which you will be able to use
  as a model for further development; and
■ contains ideas of interest to you and in which the action is
  exciting.

Plot

Think about the shape and structure of the plot in the story or poem.

- Where does the climax come?
- How does the writer make use of suspense?
- Does the writer keep the audience *guessing* by holding up the action, or by withholding some vital information about a character?
- How can you plan *your* plot so that the audience is kept waiting?

Decide what changes you are going to make in your adaptation. Are you going to change the order of events to make your script more suited to a stage presentation?

Put yourself in the position of the audience and then make your decisions.

Dialogue

Remember that the purpose of dialogue in your play is to:

- create character and establish relationships;
- carry the action forward; and
- reveal information in a natural way.

But it must not seem to be forced and unreal, i.e. the words must be as near as possible to those used by people in real life. However, because in real life people tend to speak at the same time, to interrupt each other, to change the subject, you must organise your dialogue so that it holds your audience's attention and makes the dramatic impact you are hoping to achieve.

We suggest that you:

- use only a few characters;
- decide what you are going to do with the characters who aren't talking;
- intersperse dialogue with movement and make use of pauses;
- say the dialogue aloud as you write it. Does it sound like the way people really speak? Does it sound like the way your characters would really speak? 'Listen' to the way the characters speak and think in the story. Do you notice any mismatch? Finally, will it interest your listeners?

Characters

In a play the audience comes to know the character as a result of various things.

- What he does. (If he behaves 'out of character' there must be a reason for it.)
- What he says and how he says it (dialogue is vital).
- How he reacts to other people (he won't necessarily behave in the same way to all the characters. People seldom do in real life).
- What other characters have to say about him.
- The way he dresses and moves (stage directions are important in giving such details).

Script layout

Decide how you are going to differentiate action from speech and then be consistent so that it is quite clear to your cast and to your producers.

Sometimes it will be necessary to give actors and producers some indication of the way in which a speech should be delivered. Don't overdo this. If your dialogue is realistic it will be clear how the words need to be said. In any case, if the characters are well-developed, then the cast will have their own ideas about interpretation.

The setting of your play should be made clear from the outset (i.e. time and place of action). If the story you are adapting moves in space and time you will in all probability need to decide where your play is to be set, and then move all the action to that place. This will involve making changes. Decide what they are.

Work in the process

Finally, whilst it is probably true that all writing benefits from being worked at, with script writing it is essential that you are prepared to re-write dialogue; to develop or to cut down scenes; to introduce new characters.

What follows is a short story by Geraldine O'Donnell.

The Stone

Such a day it was. A day flying on the wind. The sky, a monstrous shape, chased over the land, its air abuzz with grit and lost things, a feather, a leaf, a skittering paper. Only the lonely, the inquisitive, stood the whip of this day that had almost reached supper-time.

An old man dug in the sand by the boiling lead sea. His hands, like two crabs, walked into the flint. The wind was behind him and carried his smell to the boy who stood watching him. The boy sniffed and smelt the sweat on the ends of the old man's hairs, the dried wet in his trousers, the dark tea on his breath. In the face covered with a mildew of beard something showed reddish and wet and behind it the teeth bit towards the boy.

'Want something, boy?'

'No.'

The crabs that were hands moved deep in the sand.

'I do. You got anything, boy?'

'No.'

The eyes narrow and sharp and lively skipped over the boy.

'Not a tanner? Not a penny? P'raps a sweet? Deep in the pocket, prickly with bits from the seam?'

'No – not even a sweet.'

'You've something in that pocket of yours. You're holding something.'

'There's only me in the pocket.'

The wind came across the sea, it went through the old man's hair and stood it on end.

'Only you?' he said. 'Two hands in pockets could be just only you. But one in the pocket means you hold something you want to keep safe.'

'No – there's nothing.'

'Then show me the nothing.'

The boy, pale as the moon he'd seen set so often, moved back with the wind.

'I don't want to show you anything. I've nothing to give.'

'Then I'll show you something,' said the old man. 'Come close. Come near.'

The boy crept over the brown sugar sand that tasted of salt.

'Look here,' said the old man. 'Deep in my hand. Look.'

He opened his fingers as though they might be the petals of some rare flower, and in the gravelled palm the boy saw a stone.

Such a stone.

'Look,' said the old man and his voice was as warm as the sun, 'the stone is as round and as smooth as a watch you keep in your pocket. Dark it is, dark as the face of the moon that's turned away from the earth. And the patterns on it. Have you ever looked in the pupil of your eye? Ah! In a glass maybe, but have you ever looked in your eye with an eye? And the stone, it has the heat of your body. On a day tipped with frost you can put it in the cold of your shoe, warm your toes. This stone was made by the crust of the earth, polished by the sea and inside is the wisdom of a thousand years. You'll not find a match for it. Such a stone only comes once.'

'Where has it come from?' said the boy.

'From the sea, as far as we can tell. The sea's done with it and brought it here to our feet. Now it watches what we'll do with it.'

'What will you do with it?' said the boy.

'I'll give it away, for it's not a thing to be sold.'

'Will you give it to me?'

'I might if you take it right.'

'You mean if I say please?'

'What's that? Please? That's a word taught to a talking bird. It's the way of taking I want.'

The boy held out his hand.

'Yes – with the hand. But not that hand. The stone must be taken with the hand that's in your pocket.'

'Only my mother sees that hand.'

'If you want the stone you must take it with the hand that only your mother sees.'

The boy spoke on the wind and the words went in fragments towards the houses over the hills.

'I showed my hand once. they stared. Then they stared at the places behind I couldn't see, and that was worse. And they smiled. A special smile that's only in the mouth.'

'Do you want the stone?' said the old man.

'What else can it do? Tell me what other things it can do.'

'It'll keep the leaves green, the flowers in bud, and you'll hear the cuckoo all year round. What else do you want it to do?'

'Can it make things grow?'

'What things?'

'Things lost that won't grow again by themselves.'

'Maybe.'

'Could it make fingers grow?'

'It might. They wouldn't be fingers you could see but they'd be there all the same.'

'I don't understand.'

'Do you understand how the moon moves the sea? How the ant talks when it builds an empire?'

'No.'

'Then keep the stone close, don't sell it or swop it and it'll give you fingers.'

'So I can play tennis and cricket and things?'

'So you can know what you see in the small death of sleep. So you can hear more than the dog hears. So you can touch a ghost. So you can smell a cloud. So you can see a star that's died.'

'How do you know the stone can do those things?'

'Why do you question it, boy?'

'Because –' the boy paused, listening to the hot blood running through his head carrying remembered words of cautious adults, 'because,' he said again, and added, to hush the rushing blood, 'it's not polite to say.'

'Because,' said the old man, 'you know the word tramp. Because I'm looked at from the side of the eye. I live with the flea and the bug. I'm a piece of meat that walks the gutters inside a wooden sandwich, carrying the word of God across my navel. I comfort my buttocks in front of bakery vents. I taste what other men eat on discarded butts and root for my food in bins. I drink lilac spirit and dream wild dreams that warm the cold corners of my skin and fill my stomach up. So how could I know, boy. Eh?'

The old man, his body bent like a question mark, waited for the boy to deny him.

'That's a shameful life.'

'That's a life, boy. Can the men, as they rush past me in their boiled clothes, give themselves time to listen to the tick of thoughts? That's why I know what I know, because time hangs heavy, rich and dark as a grape, waiting for me to pluck it and taste its secrets.'

The boy raised his head, listened, and looked towards the hills. Somewhere a clock was striking. The sound wavered, then beat upon the wind. Now it was supper-time. As if the hills were glass, the boy saw through them into the windows of his home where knives and forks and spoons were being rattled and paired.

'I've go to go,' he said.

'Will you not stay awhile?' said the old man.

'No, I must go.'

'Won't you take what I have to give you?' said the old man.

'It's only a stone,' said the boy, and he turned his mind and his voice to the clock.

The boy walked lightly away, treading carefully as though he dare not leave his mark showing that he'd been there. The old man watched the wind sift sand into the frightened prints and when the beach was smooth again the old man bent the question-mark body over the crab-like hands and began again to dig.

Reading　　　　　Work in pairs and read the story. Divide the dialogue between you as if it were a play script.

Writing　　　　　Write your own play script based on this story. Make use of the guidelines and our unfinished script with its suggestions for including improvisation. Finally, give your play a suitable title.

　　　　　　　　　Write the next scene in which the boy, having returned home, is asked by his mother where he has been and with whom. You will need to consider:
- what the boy decides to tell his mother;
- the character of the mother and her attitude towards what he says.

Drama　　　　　Working in small groups, select one script for presentation to another group. As you rehearse it, make any alterations to the script which you think will make it more effective.

Work sharing and　During your work-sharing sessions evaluate the script writing
evaluation　　　under the following headings.
- Overall shape and development of plot.
- Convincing characterisation and dialogue.
- Dramatic interest and conflict.
- Suitability of setting to presentation in a small space with limited facilities.

The Stone (Working title)

(*adapted from a story by Geraldine O'Donnell*)

The Scene . . . . a seashore
Time . . . . late afternoon
Sound Effects . . . . .sea sounds, seagulls calling

Beginning I: improvisation
Any number of people can be used to convey the atmosphere of a day having been spent at the seaside, e.g.
- families with tired children and all their seaside luggage;
- day trippers from an old people's home;
- young couples armed with magazines and transistor radios;
- Punch and Judy entertainer;
- ice-cream sellers;
- balloon sellers;
- toffee apple sellers, etc.

Imagine what scraps of conversation might be heard as they prepare to leave. Write down the dialogue, then test it for realism by reading it aloud, possibly with a friend. Include some of the conversation in your final script.

or II: tape recorded sound effects and dialogue
You may decide to make a tape recording of sea sounds interspersed with dialogue in order to set the scene into which the boy comes.

[*As people drift homewards an old* MAN *(or woman) can be seen picking through discarded things on the beach. He begins to dig with his crab-like hands in the sand. Watching him, cautiously, a young* BOY *(or girl) advances towards him. The* TRAMP *does not turn round but senses that someone is close.*]

TRAMP   Want something boy?

BOY   No.

TRAMP   [*digging in the sand deeper with his hands*] I do – you got anything, boy?

BOY   No. [*Starts to move backwards away*]

TRAMP   Not a penny? Not a sweet? Deep in the pocket, prickly with bits from the seam?

BOY   No, not even a sweet.

TRAMP   You've something in that pocket of yours. You're holding something.

BOY   There's only me in the pocket.

TRAMP   Only you? Two hands in pockets could be just only you. But one in the pocket means you hold something you want to keep safe.

BOY   [*becoming more nervous*] No, there's nothing, nothing.

TRAMP   Then show me the nothing.

BOY   [*moving uneasily backwards*] I don't want to show you any- thing. I've nothing to give.
[*The* TRAMP *motions the* BOY *to come forward – meanwhile he scrapes the sand from some object in his hand.*]

TRAMP   Look here, deep in my hand. Look. [*He opens his fingers as though they might be the petals of some rare flower. In the palm of his hand, the* BOY *sees a stone.*] Look, this stone is as round and as smooth as a watch you keep in your pocket. Dark it is, dark, as the face of the moon that's turned away from the earth. And the patterns on it. This stone was made by the crust of the earth, polished by the sea and inside is the wisdom of a thousand years. Such a stone only comes once.

BOY   [*beginning to show interest*] Where has it come from?

TRAMP   From the sea as far as we can tell. The sea's done with it and brought it here to our feet. Now it watches what we'll do with it.

BOY   What will you do with it?

TRAMP   I'll give it away, for it's not a thing to be sold.

BOY   Will you give it to me?

TRAMP   I might if you take it right.

BOY   You mean if I say please?

TRAMP   What's that? Please! That's a word taught to a talking bird. It's the *way* of taking I want [*the* BOY *holds out his hand*]. Yes, with the hand. But not that hand. The stone must be taken with the hand that's in your pocket.

BOY   Only my mother sees that hand.

TRAMP   If you want the stone you must take it with the hand that only your mother sees.

BOY   I showed my hand once . . . they stared.

Improvisation

Other short scenes (flashbacks) might be introduced showing various reactions to the boy's deformed hand.

The action between the tramp and the boy will have to be suspended during this 'memory scene' — how will you achieve it?

Continue with your script. You may wish to re-write the ending.

NOVEL

Devil by the Sea, Nina Bawden

'I haven't read it, but I've seen it', is a familiar comment, pointing to the fact that many novels have been successfully adapted for film and stage presentation. Recent stage adaptations include *Animal Farm*, *Cider with Rosie*, *Nicholas Nickleby* and *Of Mice and Men*. As far as the latter is concerned, Steinbeck wrote it so that it could easily be presented in play form. A close study of any one of the chapters would show this to be true.

Perhaps the most satisfying experience is one which enables us to appreciate both the art form of the novel and the play or film script. Certainly we can all learn to appreciate what is involved in the adaptation of a novel by becoming engaged in the task.

Devil by the Sea is a gripping story involving an interesting and unusual set of characters seen through the eyes of a girl, Hilary, who is in her ninth year.

During that particular summer, she meets 'the Devil' or 'Dotty Jim', her father dies, and she is involved in a murder hunt. These events have a profound effect on her attitude and her behaviour towards the other members of her family.

The novel has all the ingredients of a compelling drama. What follows is an extract from Chapter 2 for you to read.

Charles Bray, the children's father, sat in the stuffy cubby-hole at the back of his shop with a cup of tea and the evening paper and hesitated to telephone his wife. If he telephoned her, she would laugh at him and he was afraid of her laughter.

The face of the murdered child stared up at him from the badly printed page. She had lost one of her milk teeth and the gap gave her face a sentimental innocence that her eyes denied. They were bright eyes with a clear, knowing look: she was a very self-conscious little beauty. Dressed in her party frock, she had posed for the camera artfully, turning slightly away so that you could see the childish line of her cheek, the loveliness of bone beneath the baby flesh. He saw, briefly, what she might have grown into: the pretty blonde from the London slum, a rose in the gutter, the boys mad about her. Her name had been Camelia, Camelia Perkins. Wondering what wild and hopeless fantasy had inspired her christening, he thought the grand name made her ugly death seem even more pointless and absurd, a kind of cosmic joke.

He stubbed out his cigarette and swore at himself. He was being foolish. Death had given this sad child no significance: it had only finished the promise of those eyes. She was not important any more. Only the living mattered, his children with a madman loose in the town. His panic mounted. He stretched out his hand and slowly dialled the number of his house.

The telephone rang once and Alice answered it. 'Is anything the matter, dear?'

'You're not busy?' he inquired nervously. She was frequently impatient when he telephoned her: her day, she sometimes hinted, was a good deal more fully occupied than his.

'No, dear. I've just had a bath.'

He pictured her, sitting at her dressing-table, talking into the white telephone receiver and watching herself in the glass.

He said flatly, 'You remember that child who was missing two days ago? The little girl?'

'Have they found her?'

'In one of those filthy huts on the flats. She was murdered.'

'How dreadful,' she said in an interested, bright voice. 'Is it all in the papers?'

'Yes. In the evening papers. Alice . . .' He cleared his throat. 'Are the children home?'

He heard her chuckle softly. 'No, Charles. They're on the beach. But nothing can happen to them. They're with Janet, quite safe.'

'I suppose Janet is responsible?' A new worry nagged his mind. 'You know what young girls are. Running about after boys.'

'Not Janet, dear. She's a nice, sheltered, hockey-playing schoolgirl. She knows nothing about sex except what she learned in Botany.'

'Perhaps you're right. She doesn't mind looking after the children, does she?'

There was an edge to her voice. 'Why should she? When *I* was seventeen, I'd been earning my living for three years. And looking after an invalid mother.'

'I know, dear. I'm sorry.' He felt deeply guilty about his wife's early life. She had had a terrible childhood and he could not bear to think about it. She had only to mention it to gain the moral advantage in any disagreement between them.

Alice went on. 'Now, Charles, you must promise me not to worry over the children. They'll be home quite soon. I'll telephone you if you like. But you mustn't get worked up for nothing. It's bad for you.'

Her voice, indulgent and reproving, set his teeth on edge. The blood rushed to his forehead. 'Do you call murder nothing? It seems to me . . .'

The door of his cubby-hole opened and Miss Hubback, his assistant, peered at him inquiringly. He beckoned her in and she squeezed past his desk to the pile of school atlases that were stacked in the corner. She was a heavily built young woman whose drooping breasts, beneath a nylon blouse, were inadequately enclosed in a pink, spotted brassiere. The effect was neither provocative nor pretty. As she bent over the atlases, Charles saw an expanse of fat, pale thigh. One of her stocking seams was twisted. Charles averted his eyes.

Alice said patiently, 'What were you going to say, dear? *Must* you say, "it seems to me"? It's becoming such a silly habit.' He knew that her face had assumed a sweet, martyred expression. 'Now, Charles, I'm just as worried as you are. You know how terribly I worry over the children. But I *force* myself to control it. For their sakes. It's so bad for them to feel that you're worried on their behalf. It destroys their sense of security.'

Miss Hubback tiptoed elaborately back to the shop. Before she closed the door she smiled at Charles brightly, showing her strong teeth.

Alice continued, 'So you're not to be a silly old hen. Think of your blood pressure. The children won't be long. I'll go and watch for the bus as soon as I've made myself decent. And I'll let you know the moment they're safely home. Will that do?'

'Yes,' he said. 'That'll do. Thank you.' He wondered why he was thanking her. Perhaps because it was nice of her to humour him.

He said, 'I'm sorry if you think I'm being an ass.'

'Not an ass, darling. Just an old fussbudget. But I love you.'

It was only a gesture, he thought, a habit, like asking people how they were when really you didn't care at all.

He said, 'I love you, too,' and put the telephone down. He was conscious of feeling tired, the way he had often felt tired lately when he had been talking to Alice. It was as if an enormous physical effort had been asked of him and his body had to call upon all its reserves of energy. He longed for peace.

It was odd, he thought, because Alice wasn't particularly difficult. She was a good sort and she didn't nag, except very occasionally. And anyway, he loved her. He must hang on to that: he loved his wife.

He looked at the letter lying on his desk and the murder went out of his mind. His rates had been put up in the last assessment: they were three times what they had been when he had taken over the bookshop at the end of the war. As things stood at the moment, to pay them would just about cripple him. He supposed he could appeal: he wondered what good it would do. He brushed his hand over his eyes and thrust the demand into an open drawer among the other unpaid bills. He would think about it to-morrow. He got up heavily and went into the shop.

*

Replacing the receiver, Alice smiled at herself in the glass. Charles was getting to the difficult age, she thought, he took everything so hard. If he wasn't worrying about the children, he was worrying about his health or about the business. He walked through life suspiciously, beset by imaginary dangers on every side.

She picked up a brush and painted her lips carefully. The silver charms tinkled on the bracelet on her wrist. Her raised, bare arm was shapely, the flesh smooth and covered with freckles. As she outlined her eyes with a dark pencil, she thought about the murder and about the empty field behind the house, dense with long grass and scrubby thorn bushes. It had been bought by a speculative builder at the beginning of the summer and he was waiting for his licence. Anyone could approach the back of the house without being seen. Perhaps there was already someone there, waiting and watching.

The pulse jumped in her throat. Her wide, alarmed eyes stared back at her from the tinted mirror. How silly and thoughtless of Charles to alarm her so. He knew how imaginative she was . . . .

She stood up and regarded herself critically in the glass, her lips pursed. The grey dress fitted her perfectly, the soft wool flowed easily over her breasts and hips. She was a big woman and needed to dress carefully. She twisted round to see that her stocking seams were straight and touched her braided hair. A small, pleased smile flickered on her lips.

She left her bedroom and went slowly down the stairs. A floor creaked and her heart raced. Muttering under her breath, she went into the kitchen, shut and bolted the back door. The action stirred up panic: she ran from room to room, closing and locking the windows against the chill air of the dying summer. She stood in the hall, her hand to her heart, listening to the ticking of the clock.

The stillness came alive around her. Whispering sounds menaced her from every room. Perhaps she had locked the door too late, perhaps there was already someone in the house? She was alone except for Auntie, resting in her room. And Auntie, Charles's Aunt Florence, would never have heard an intruder: she was deaf as a post. Intractable, old and proud, she refused to admit this failing of her senses although for years she had heard no sounds but the ringing bells inside her own head.

Thinking of this, an ancient resentment stirred. Why should Auntie be allowed to keep her eccentric illusion just because her father had been a knight? Anger drove out fear.

'Don't be a bloody fool,' Alice said aloud. She never swore in public, being anxious, above all things, to appear well bred, but when she was alone she frequently abused herself with violent expressions and found they comforted her. 'You silly, neurotic bitch,' she said. The sound of her voice pleased and calmed her. Her pulses resumed their normal, regular beat.

Glancing at her watch, she left the house and walked to the front gate, looking across the Downs to the wide sea. Peebles was one of single line of houses built high on the cliff top with an uninterrupted view of the sea and, in summer, of the long line of yellow sewage that appeared, bubbling beyond the outer limits of the tide. The road was called The Way. The houses were big and rambling, Gothic in conception: at the time of their construction they had been thought rather grand houses. When Alice had been a child, the road had been a fashionable place to live. The best people in Henstable lived on The Way: at Christmas-time, the best parties had been given there and they were always the parties Alice had not been invited to. She used to walk up and down the road after dark, an angry child, loving and hating the people in the houses, watching the lighted windows and listening to the laughter. That was how she was always to feel: the good things happened on the other side of the wall.

Now the grandeur of the houses had diminished. They were merely large and inconvenient and shabby, the gardens impossible to maintain. They expressed, in their peeling paint, their dusty chandeliers, a whole chapter of middle-class decay. There were no more parties. The only rich household left belonged to Miss Fleery-Carpenter and she was old, potty, lived on boiled onions and the daily expectation of the Second Coming of Christ. Apart from the Brays, the owners of the houses were old, mostly retired people, barely conscious, though they discreetly let rooms in summer and grumbled about rising prices, that the world had changed. Occasionally they would remark to each other that people 'of their sort' did not live in Henstable any more.

But to Alice Bray, who had been Alice Parker, the bright, disciplined child from the slum houses at the other end of the town, it still seemed, for most of the time, a considerable achievement to be living on The Way. She, who had run the streets, been beaten by a drunken father, been abandoned by him at the age of fourteen, left in sole care of a paralysed, whining mother, now owned a car, sent her children to expensive schools, voted Conservative.

Smiling and well-nourished, she stood at the gate of her comfortable, shabby house and looked down the hill towards the town. From where she stood she could see the beach, the flags on the roof of the bandstand, and the long finger of the pier pointing out to sea. The sea was calm and blue, the blue sky swept down to meet it: it was a beautiful day.

As she watched, a tiny, toy bus left the pier and crawled slowly along the front. It was the four o'clock bus, the one the children usually caught when they had been on the beach. In a moment or two it would reach the foot of the hill and she could telephone Charles, tell him that the children were safe and go out to tea.

She hoped that the children had heard nothing of the trouble in the town. She must warn Janet to say nothing to them. Peregrine would not understand what had happened but Hilary was precocious and excitable: she would see at once the dramatic possibilities in the situation and use them to the full. Once she knew about the murder, she would be impossible for weeks.

The bus stopped at the bottom of the hill. She saw Janet and the children get out, three small, distant figures in cherry-coloured cardigans. She went into the house.

Miss Hubback answered the telephone. She sounded breathless. 'Oh, it's you, Mrs Bray. I'm afraid Mr Bray's busy.

We've got a traveller in. Would you like him to ring you back? You know,' she ended archly, 'how he hates to be disturbed.'

This familiarity annoyed Alice. She wished that Charles would find an assistant who was a lady. Miss Hubback had a common accent and Alice was sensitive to accents.

She said coldly, 'I'm in a hurry.'

Miss Hubback was breezy. 'Oh dear. I'd better get him then, hadn't I?'

There was a chink as she laid the telephone down. Alice could hear her humming softly as she left the tiny office. Then Charles's voice said, 'Are they all right?'

'Of course they are, dear. They've just got off the bus.'

'Good. I'm sorry if I worried you.'

'That's all right, dear. But I'm late for my little tea-party now, so would you do a small errand for me? I ordered a lobster from Goring and I haven't had time to pick it up. Do you mind?'

'Of course not. Why lobster?'

'The Wallaces are coming to dinner. Now don't say this is the first you've heard of it because I told you last week.' She put on a soft, coaxing voice. 'And, sweetheart, I know they're not really your sort of people but they really are such an interesting creative couple. So do try and be nice to them, won't you?'

'I'll be polite, I hope.'

'Of course you will. You always are, dear. But I want you to be more than polite, really friendly.'

His voice was suddenly testy. 'Wallace is in advertising, isn't he? What's creative about that?'

'He's a very clever artist, dear. And Erna Wallace is so clever with her hands. She makes pots. Really interesting, modern ones.'

'Does she now? Well, well . . .' He cleared his throat. 'All right, dear. I'll come home with the lobster. Enjoy your tea.'

She put the telephone down. There was a thumping noise on the floor above. The ceiling shuddered and, in the dining-room, the glasses on the sideboard danced against each other with a sound like little bells. Auntie was getting up after her rest. Her massive footsteps trod across the upstairs landing to the bathroom. It was like a mountain moving. She turned on the bath and began to sing in her strong, melodious voice, 'When I survey the Wondrous Cross.' Mingling with the splashing water, her voice rose painfully to the high note beyond her range and sank, gladly, to a swelling contralto. 'On which the Prince of Glo-ry di-ed.'

'Stupid old fool,' said Alice loudly. Auntie had been living at Peebles for over a year and Alice felt she would never become used to her presence. Since her arrival, a distinct musty smell had hung about the bedroom floor and the old woman made unpleasant noises in the bathroom. Although she was rich, she never offered to contribute towards the household expenses. Alice had, on several occasions, discussed the rising cost of living in her presence but she had not taken the hint. On the other hand, Charles was her favourite nephew . . . .

'Mummy,' Hilary called. 'Mummy.' Her voice was high and eager. She ran in at the gate but when she saw her mother she stopped abruptly and stood uneasily still, rubbing one dusty sandal up and down the back of her leg. Her face took on an expression of dumb idiocy.

Alice knew that Hilary was pleased to see her and too shy to show it, nevertheless she was irritated, as always, by the child's inability to express an attractive emotion.

She said, 'What a mess you're in. Surely you don't have to get so dirty?'

Hilary squirmed her shoulders and did not answer. Peregrine came up to Alice, carrying a pail full of shells.

'Look,' he said, 'I've got lots of pink ones. I'm going to make a necklace for your birthday.'

There were dark rings of tiredness round his eyes. His cheeks were flushed with a pale, delicate colour.

'Are you, love?' Alice kissed him lightly on the top of his head. Feeling Hilary's smouldering eyes upon her, she said, 'Did you collect any shells, darling?'

'Yes. I threw them away, though. Nasty, dirty things.' Hilary exaggerated her disgust. 'Dead fish's houses.'

Janet said, 'She emptied them all over the promenade. It was a filthy mess, all mixed up with sand and seaweed. And *I* had to clean it up.' She looked hot and cross, her mouth was sullen. Alice felt annoyed: surely it wasn't too much for the girl to take the children out occasionally? She did nothing else except her silly, part-time job as secretary to the local dentist: she had no particular talents.

Alice said sweetly, 'What a bore for you. You won't mind giving them their tea, will you? It's all ready. I expect Hilary will be a good girl and help, won't you, Hilary?'

Hilary scowled and squinted down her nose.

'For heaven's sake, child, take that look off your face.'

Hilary gave her mother a bitter glance and hopped on one foot into the house, leaving a trail of damp sand behind her. Following, Peregrine carried his pail tenderly, like a chalice.

Janet said in a detached voice, 'Hilary is much fonder of you than Peregrine is. You wouldn't think it, would you?'

Alice wondered if this was intended as a reproach (she knew she was often harsher with her daughter than with Peregrine because she loved her more) but decided at once that it was unlikely. Janet was much too anxious that Alice should approve of her to be critical: sometimes her evident devotion had touched Alice's intelligence though it never had, and never could, touch her heart. Still, the knowledge of it had softened her exchanges with her stepdaughter and made it easier for her to tolerate her stupidity and lack of grace. Lately, however, Alice had fancied that Janet's attitude towards her had curiously changed: her manner had become a good deal less humble, and, at the same time, almost excessively considerate. Occasionally she would fuss over Alice as if she were someone quite old and frail: with gentle autocracy she forbade her to sit in draughts. Alice had been amused, but only to a point. That point was reached on the day that she surprised a look of pity on the girl's face. She had told herself that it was inconceivable that Janet should be sorry for her. Nevertheless the fleeting expression had affected her like an insult. From that moment, a new tartness had crept into their relationship.

Now Janet said, 'I'm sorry. That was a beastly thing to say to you.' The clumsy apology implied condescension.

Alice said coldly, 'Please do not trouble to explain my own child to me.'

The unfairness of this remark worried her briefly after Janet had gone, silent and rebuked, into the house. Then she looked at her watch, saw that she was really very late, now, and went out to tea.

Talking and writing

Consider the problems of adapting this particular extract *for stage presentation*. Make notes on your discussion and include the following issues.

■ How are you going to solve the problem of there being at least three locations?

■ What kind of acting space would best suit your purposes?

■ Would you omit any of the characters mentioned?

■ Are there any incidents or characters that you would further develop for dramatic effect?

■ How will you convey both the passing of time and Alice's mounting anxiety between the telephone calls?

List the characters in order of appearance, making full use of the clues given; write brief notes such as would help actors and actresses to play their parts.

Plan and draw the set.

What major differences would you expect to find between a stage and a television adaptation of this extract? Mention some techniques and devices that could be used in a television presentation.

Draw a storyboard for part or all of this extract (see page 55) for guidance). Decide which incidents to include and the order in which you want them to appear so that you obtain the maximum dramatic effect. For example, you could begin with a scene on the beach zooming into a close up of two children playing in the sand. A man watches from a distance. The second frame might show Charles Bray, the children's father, reading a newspaper; the third a close up of the face of the murdered child.

A play for voices

We chose to adapt the novel as a play for voices which could be presented on radio or staged simply in the round using a few symbolic props.

Included here is the first draft of the script which covers some of the events in Chapter 2.

List of characters
Charles Bray
Alice Bray
Alice's imaginary voices
Florence (Charles Bray's aged aunt)
Hilary Bray (daughter, aged 9 years)
Peregrine Bray (son – aged 7 years)
Janet Bray (Charles Bray's daughter – aged 17 years)

The Telephone Call

[*Telephone rings in the Bray household.*]

ALICE [*picks up phone, recognises her husband's voice.*]   Is there anything the matter, dear?

CHARLES   You're not busy?

ALICE   No, dear. I've just had a bath.

CHARLES   You remember that child who was missing two days ago? The little girl?

ALICE   Have they found her?

CHARLES   In one of those filthy huts on the flats. She was murdered.

ALICE [*interested bright voice.*]   How dreadful. Is it in all the papers?

CHARLES   Yes. In the evening papers. Alice. [*Pause.*] Are the children home?

ALICE   No, Charles. They're on the beach. But nothing can happen to them. They're with Janet, quite safe.

CHARLES   I suppose Janet is responsible? You know what young girls are. Running about after boys.

ALICE   Not Janet, dear. She's a nice, sheltered, hockey-playing schoolgirl. She knows nothing about sex except what she learned in Botany.

CHARLES   Perhaps you're right. She doesn't mind looking after the children, does she?

ALICE [*harshly.*]   Why should she? When *I* was seventeen, I'd been earning my living for three years. And looking after an invalid mother.

CHARLES   I know, dear. I'm sorry.

ALICE   Now, Charles, you must promise not to worry over the children. They'll be home quite soon. I'll telephone you if you like. But you mustn't get worked up for nothing. It's bad for you.

CHARLES   Do you call murder nothing? It seems to me . . .

ALICE   What were you saying, dear? *Must* you say 'It seems to me'? It's becoming such a silly habit. Now, Charles, I'm just as worried as you are. You know how terribly I worry over the children. But I *force* myself to control it. For their sakes. It's so bad for them to feel that you're worried on their behalf. It destroys their sense of security.

CHARLES   I suppose . . .

ALICE   So you're not to be a silly old hen. Think of your blood pressure. The children won't be long, I'll let you know the

143

moment they're safely home. Will that do?

CHARLES   Yes. That'll do. Thank you. I'm sorry if you think I'm being an ass.

ALICE   Not an ass, darling. Just an old fusspot. Goodbye for now.

CHARLES   Goodbye Alice [*puts the phone down*].

*

[ALICE *stands in front of imaginary mirror applying lipstick. Hall clock chimes; the* VOICES *in her head begin to whisper.*]

VOICE 1   Why did you lock the back door, Alice?

VOICE 2   Could it be too late, Alice?

VOICE 3   Is there already someone in the house?

ALICE   Of course there is, there's Auntie Florence. Charles' Aunt Florence.

VOICE 4   But Florence is deaf, 'deaf as a post' are the words you use, Alice.

ALICE [*to* ALICE]   Oh, don't be a bloody fool . . . silly neurotic bitch . . . [*Thumping noise from above as* AUNT FLORENCE *moves in her room.*]

FLORENCE [*singing voice, sinking and swelling.*]   When I survey the wondrous cross, on which the Prince of Glo-ory di-ied.

ALICE [*forced to listen.*]   Stupid old fool.

HILARY [*calling.*]   Mummy, mummy.

ALICE   What a mess you're in. Surely you don't have to get so dirty.

PEREGRINE [*holding out shells.*]   Look. I've got lots of pink ones. I'm going to make a necklace for your birthday.

ALICE   Are you, love? [*To* HILARY.] Did you collect any shells, darling?

HILARY   Yes. I threw them away, though. Nasty, dirty things. Dead fish's houses.

JANET   She emptied them all over the promenade. It was a filthy mess, all mixed up with sand and seaweed. And *I* had to clean it up.

ALICE   What a bore for you. You won't mind giving them their tea, will you? It's ready. I expect Hilary will be a good girl and help, won't you, Hilary? [*To* HILARY.] For heaven's sake, child, take that look off your face.

JANET   Hilary is much fonder of you than Peregrine is. You wouldn't think it, would you? [*Pause.*] I'm sorry. That was a beastly thing to say to you.

ALICE   Please do not trouble to explain my own child to me.

Drama

Working in small groups, rehearse the script. Experiment with suitable sound effects and appropriate music. Now, make your tape recording.

Share your work with other groups. Comment on any differences of interpretation and treatment.

Talking

After re-reading the extract from the novel, discuss what you think is lost in this instance, through adaptation into a script.

This drawing was produced by an artist after he had read our play script. Discuss its effectiveness as a book cover in relation to the extract you have read.

PICTORIAL
Creative writing from a visual stimulus

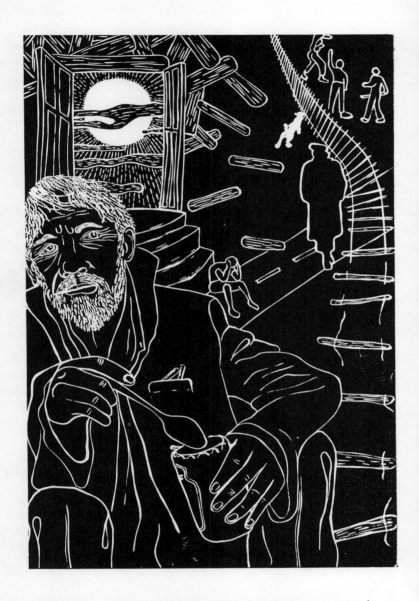

As part of your examination in English and Drama, you may be given a drawing or photograph as a stimulus for creative writing in verse, prose or drama.

Writing

Use any part or all of the visual stimulus material as a basis for your writing.

Begin by jotting down *all* the ideas which occur to you in any order.

Select one of your ideas for development as a poem, short story or drama script. Give your work an interesting title.

7

Fact, feeling, form

The story of Charlotte Dymond

In this chapter we draw together our experience of different forms of literature by looking at the range of newspaper and magazine writing, poetry, melodrama and T.V. documentary drama generated by one story, a murder which took place in the nineteenth century.

Apart from the interest you will find in reading, talking and writing about the different forms of the extracts, you will have some source material upon which to base a documentary of your own.

It would be a mistake to assume that newspapers are all fact and that poetry is all feeling. The documentary genre gives us an opportunity to work with material from a variety of sources and to shape and organise it so that it expresses a personal or group viewpoint.

Here are two extracts, the first from *True Crime Monthly* magazine and the second from *The Times* newspaper, 1 May 1844, which tell the stories of the murder of Charlotte Dymond and the trial of Matthew Weeks.

Dreadful Murder

Penhale farm lies a couple of miles from Davidstow on the northern edge of the moor. 140 years ago it was the scene of one of the greatest of Victorian cases. The ghastly bloodletting made front page news across the country and even the Times carried the story . . .

The Death certificate of Charlotte Dymond showed the cause of death as wilful murder by Weeks some three and a half months before his trial

S HE LAY on her back, her pretty green gown open to the stomach, immodestly revealing her plump thighs. She lay a foot away from a small moorland stream, one arm outstretched, a leg bent comfortably, face turned towards the sky. She might have been gazing up at the passing clouds, lost in some pastoral reverie – but for the obvious fact that her throat had been cut.

The mystery of the nine-day disappearance of 18-year-old servant girl Charlotte Dymond had been solved. The other mystery – who killed her? – seemed to have been solved even before her body was found. Matthew Weeks, aged 23, a fellow-servant in the same household, had already been judged and found guilty by his neighbours. All that remained was the formality of a trial . . . .

The instrinsic value of the Charlotte Dymond case is that it serves as a kind of time-capsule, affording us a valuable glimpse into the past. We can see how justice was administered in 1844 – even learn something of the lives of ordinary people then.

The Story Began ...

It began on a farm called Penhale, owned by Phillipa Peter, a 61-year-old widow. Together with her unmarried son John and three servants, she ran the 147-acre holding from a large stone house a couple of miles away from Davidstow, a village on the northern edge of Bodmin Moor, which had both a church and a Methodist chapel. Matthew Weeks was the principal farmhand, having worked at Penhale for some seven years. He had pock-marked, sullen features and was lame in his right leg. When he smiled, he revealed a gap-toothed mouth – and his only good feature was a mop of curly light-brown hair. He had lately been 'keeping company' with Charlotte Dymond, who had a reputation as a flirt.

On Lady Day, March 25th – the day servants were hired and fired – Charlotte was paid-off by Mrs Peter after 18 months of service. She received four shillings in change, which included two silver fourpenny pieces. But since she had nowhere else to go, she remained at the farm for the time being.

Taken on to replace her was 21-year-old John Stevens, who seemed to spend his time spying on Matthew Weeks. This was not difficult, since both shared a bedroom. Stevens was quick to note that Weeks owned both a knife and a cut-throat razor. He also noted the jealousy existing between Weeks and a man called Thomas Prout, who had boasted that he would take Charlotte away from Weeks. Indeed, Stevens witnessed a bitter row between Weeks and Prout over Charlotte.

On the afternoon of Sunday, April 14th, Charlotte and Matthew Weeks dressed in their best finery – Charlotte in a green gown, with red shawl, brown silk bonnet and black handbag – and set off for a walk. Matthew Weeks returned alone at 9.30 that evening. When asked where Charlotte was, he replied: 'I don't know.' He then went to bed.

The following morning, after he got up to pursue his normal activities around the farm, Mrs Peter went up to make his bed. She was surprised to find his stockings, which she had put out clean the day before, covered in mud up to the knees. His best trousers, too, were muddy. When a suspicious Mrs Peter questioned Weeks about his movements the day before, he said he had walked with Charlotte as far as Higher Down Gate, some three-quarters of a mile from the farmhouse. And there they had parted, she to walk on in the direction of Bodmin Moor, he to walk to a village in the opposite direction.

With each day that passed, with no sign of Charlotte, gossip mounted. Local farmer Isaac Cory had seen Matthew Weeks walking with Charlotte on the Sunday, a good deal further out on the moor than Higher Down Gate. The couple had been wearing *pattens*, metal undershoes which, strapped to one's boots, kept them clear of the mud. They also left a distinctive oval pattern in the turf, which Isaac Cory had spotted.

On the Tuesday of April 16th, an increasingly-worried Mrs Peter decided to tackle Weeks about the missing girl, threatening to bring him before a magistrate if he did not tell the truth. It was then that he mumbled an explanation. Charlotte, having found a new position at a place called Blisland, had gone there on the Sunday. Since she couldn't travel so far in one day, she had intended breaking her journey by sleeping out on the moor. It was a flimsy tale. For why would Charlotte have walked out with only what she stood up in, leaving all her other clothing behind?

By Saturday, April 20th, the gossip was at a height, with men in public houses openly baiting Weeks, though stopping just short of accusing him of murder. During this period, John Stevens saw two silver fourpenny pieces in Weeks's possession. Mrs Peter had not paid Weeks with such coins. Once again, his employer tackled Weeks about the missing girl, telling him that, if he had indeed done away with the girl, he ought to be 'hung in chains'.

On Sunday, April 21st, when Matthew Weeks went out, Mrs Peter took the opportunity to thoroughly search his room. In the jacket he had worn on the day Charlotte disappeared, she found a handkerchief belonging to Charlotte. And his razor seemed to be missing ...

Matthew Weeks did not return to the farm. He had fled the district, perhaps fearing that his story about Charlotte – that she had gone to a family called Laxton at Blisland – was about to be branded a lie. John Stevens had been sent to check – and the Laxtons had told him that they had never seen Charlotte, nor offered her a position.

Two days later – with local opinion satisfied of his guilt – it was decided to scout the moor for his supposed victim's body. The search party followed patten prints in the moorland turf, measuring the length of them by notching a stick. The prints eventually ran out on rocky ground, where the searchers divided into two groups. In the marshy area around Roughtor, Simon Baker and William Northam stumbled across the body of Charlotte. Missing from the body were the bonnet, shoes and pattens, handkerchief, wool shawl, handbag and gloves. Some 50 yards away, the searchers found more patten marks in the marshy ground, as if a couple had stood face-to-face. One set matched the measurement notched on the stick.

Surgeon's Report

The surgeon's report later stated: 'I found a wound in the neck eight and a half inches in length. The windpipe was completely divided at its upper part, including a small portion of the larynx. The oesophagus was partly divided and the instrument had not only gone through the soft part, but had partially separated two of the vertebrae by entering a little way into the cartilage between them. Much force must have been used in giving the wound .... The wound was the cause of death. I do not think the instrument used was a very sharp one .... I do not think she could have inflicted the wound herself. I examined the rest of the body, which was healthy. The bladder was empty, but this might have happened after death. The uterus was healthy and there were no signs of pregnancy, or violation .... The hymen was ruptured, but the rupture did not appear to be recent.'

The Inquest

Next came the inquest. The coroner was Joseph Hamley, himself a surgeon. His son Edmund, a solicitor, acted as deputy. Witnesses and jury members had been arriving at the farm all day. In all, 19 witnesses gave evidence, including Isaac Cory, who had seen Charlotte with Weeks on the moor. There was also local preacher William Gard, who had actually seen a couple on Roughtor at the relevant time. The man had appeared to be lame.

Richard Pethwick, a local farmer, had also been riding on the moor on that Sunday. He had spoken to the couple, asking them if they were lost. 'The man was lame,' he related. Then the physical evidence was produced. The broken coral necklace, a shirt belonging to Weeks, with blood-stains on it – and Charlotte's handkerchief, which had been found in his pocket.

Without adjourning, the jury brought in their verdict: '... That Matthew Weeks, late of the parish aforesaid ... not having the fear of God before his eyes, but moved and seduced by the instigation of the Devil ... did murder Charlotte Dymond.' Within 24 hours of this verdict, the coroner had issued a death certificate for Charlotte, giving the cause of death as: 'Wilfully murdered by Matthew Weeks.' He also issued a warrant for the arrest of Matthew Weeks.

The Arrest

Constable John Bennett set off in pursuit of the fugitive. He soon discovered that Matthew Weeks had visited the Stevens family – some 10 miles from Penhale Farm – on the day he fled. He arrived about 3 o'clock and left at 9 p.m., having spent those six hours chatting to two girls – Elizabeth Stevens and her friend Eliza Butler. Not knowing of Charlotte's disappearance, but knowing of her engagement to Weeks, they had asked after her. Weeks had answered their questions readily, displaying no unease. He had seemed very calm and relaxed. At one point, he even took from his pocket Charlotte's black handbag to show them.

'The wound was inflicted with great force – the sort a person might inflict upon himself'

The trail led Bennett to Plymouth – Weeks had a sister living there – and he was in fact arrested at his sister's house. After being told that he was being charged with the murder of Charlotte

Dymond, his clothing was searched. In a side-pocket were found a pair of gloves belonging to Charlotte. Asked what he was doing in Plymouth, Weeks replied that he had hoped to take passage on a ship to Jersey. Questioned about his relations with Charlotte, he said he had not 'kept company with Charlotte since Lady Day, but some other chaps had.'

The Hearing

All Drunkard Inn, Halworthy, where magistrates heard the case against Weeks

By April 25th, Weeks had been returned to Davidstow to face the magistrates. The hearing took place in a local inn, with Weeks handcuffed to a steel bar which ran from floor to ceiling. All the original inquest witnesses were called to report their evidence – and the various forensic items were produced once again.

Weeks, who pleaded not guilty, had no real defence. Indeed, the evidence seemed damning. Even his statement to a solicitor seemed contrived. In that statement, he admitted that he had gone for a walk with Charlotte that fateful Sunday, but denied having murdered her. His statement read: 'I went along with her a little way ... and then she said she did not want me to go any further. I wished her well and bade her good afternoon. She left me and I left her.' This statement had been dictated – he could neither read nor write – and the wording was obviously that of the solicitor.

No doubt it was not justice as we perceive it today. Weeks had no opportunity to defend himself – an accused man was not able to speak on his own behalf – he had been branded a murderer by the coroner's death certificate and found guilty by the local press. But all his actions had been consistent with guilt, so it was not surprising that the magistrates found he had a charge to answer. They had him lodged in Bodmin gaol to await the next assize court.

Missing Clothing Found

While Weeks languished in his cell, the moor was searched for Charlotte's missing clothing. Isaac Cory and his wife eventually found them hidden in a two-foot-deep pit, half a mile from where the body was found. Constable Rickard witnessed the find. Hidden under moss in the pit were the missing items belonging to Charlotte – her shoes, shawl, bonnet – and the steel pattens she had been wearing. The constable also found something else of significance. Searching the stream bank, close to where the body was found, he noticed a loose clump of turf. Upon lifting the turf, he found a hole beneath, containing a great quantity of blood.

By Tuesday, April 30th, the case was national news, with the *Morning Chronicle* headline of: DREADFUL MURDER IN CORNWALL. Even the *Times* carried the story.

The Trial

The Bodmin assize trial of Matthew Weeks began on Friday, August 2nd, 1844. Frederick William Slade was his defence counsel, while Alexander Cockburn, QC, led for the Crown. Mr Justice Patteson presided. First, though, a special grand jury had to consider whether, on the evidence, a 'true bill' had been proved against Matthew Weeks. It was, in effect, a pre-trial hearing. Had the grand jury returned a verdict of *ignoramus*, there would have been no trial. But the 23-man grand jury returned a verdict of 'true' – and, from that moment, Weeks faced a trial proper for his life.

The judge took his seat in the packed courtroom, after which the prisoner was put in the dock. As the indictment was read to him, he replied in a low voice: 'Not guilty'. Then Alexander Cockburn made his opening address. He went through the story, piece by piece – Charlotte's disappearance, the muddy trousers of Weeks, his flight from justice. He would prove wilful murder, he said.

Witnesses For The Prosecution

One by one, the witnesses were called. Those who had found the body described the scene – no blood either on the ground or the body, no signs of a struggle. Dr Good told how the wound was deeper on the left side than the right, inference being that the assailant must have attacked Charlotte from the front, presuming that he was right-handed. He went on to say: 'The wound was inflicted with great force, probably with a knife.'

However, under cross-examination from the defence, Good admitted that since the body had lain sloping downwards, with the head facing the stream, such a cut would have drained all the blood from the veins directly into the water. He added: 'It was the sort of wound a person might inflict on himself.'

The prosecution re-examined. Was it *likely* that Charlotte had cut her own throat? 'I think it's possible, but not likely,' the doctor replied. 'I am not prepared to say, with reference to the extent, how much of such a wound a person could inflict upon himself.' He agreed that she could have been killed a little away from the stream, then carried there. But this raised the vexed question of *why had there been no blood found on Weeks's clothing?* If he had cut her throat from in front, or carried her, then he must have received some bloodstains. Yet he had not. . . .

The witnesses who had seen Charlotte with Weeks on Roughtor, less than 100 yards from where her body was found, proved particularly damning. Isaac Cory had seen the couple, while Richard Pethwick had spoken to them. The latter was now prepared to state: 'I swear that the prisoner was the man beyond belief.'

For The Defence

Finally, at about 7 p.m., Frederick Slade rose to put the defence case. He spoke for only an hour, in contrast to the prosecution's nine and a half hours. But then, there was so little he *could* say . . . . He complained that the press had created a bias against his client, which must affect the jury's decision. He declared that the Crown had failed to establish any motive. Nor had they proved that Weeks had ever had possession of a knife, nor shown him to have any of the bloodstains on his clothing, which *must* have showered the real murderer – if indeed it *was* a murder . . . . It was entirely possible that, after Matthew Weeks left her, Charlotte Dymond had met another man on the moor – perhaps by prior arrangement – who then killed her. As for his client's 'flight from justice,' it was a reasonable action to walk out of the farm, in view of the local suspicion and hostility. In short, the Crown's case was purely circumstantial.

The Summing Up

When he sat down, Mr Justice Patteson began to sum up the evidence. It was impossible to believe that Charlotte could have inflicted the wound upon herself, he said. And while the Crown had failed to show any motive for the murder, Weeks had been identified as the last person seen in her company. 'It is a case of circumstances entirely. Nobody saw him commit the act, if he *did* do it. Circumstantial evidence is always to be very carefully and cautiously examined, for there is nothing so apt to deceive one. And how easy it is to dovetail a number of circumstances together and fancy that a very clear case is made out when, in truth, it is not so!'

'I took out my knife and went towards her to commit the bloody deed . . . . I approached behind her and made a cut at her throat . . . . She fell back, the blood gushing out in a large stream . . . '

Nevertheless, it has often been said that circumstantial evidence, if well-weighed and examined, is often more satisfactory than direct testimony because, in direct testimony, a motive may be *suspected*. Whereas, in circumstances, there is often no doubt at all. When they are put together and examined and compared, they tell a story which cannot lead to direct falsehood.'

The judge finished his summing-up just before 10 p.m.

The Verdict

And the jury retired for 35 minutes, before returning with a verdict of guilty. The black cap was placed on the judge's head as he addressed himself to the prisoner. 'Matthew Weeks, the jury, after a very full and patient investigation of this case, have come to the conclusion that you are guilty of the offence with which you are charged, having murdered the poor girl Charlotte Dymond . . . . The circumstances of this case do not disclose to the jury or to me the motive which induced you to commit the offence . . . . The time you will pass in this world is now very short. Your age is very young. Still, that does not justify me in holding out the slightest hope that the extreme sentence of the law will not be carried out in your case – and that there will be any mercy shown to you.

'There being no hope for you in this world, my earnest entreaty is for you to endeavour to obtain that mercy from the Almighty, which man cannot grant you .... You shall be taken hence to the place from whence you came and be hung by the neck until you are dead. Your body shall be buried within the precincts of the prison. May the Lord have mercy on your soul.'

Even before he finished speaking, Weeks had fainted.

The Execution

Monday, August 12th, 1844 – an estimated 20,000 people gathered outside the prison to watch the execution. As the clock struck midday, Weeks was led out of the prison gate, his arms pinioned. The governor and the chaplain accompanied him, the latter reading a prayer as the procession made its way to the scaffold. According to contemporary press reports, Weeks could barely walk, with 'the little strength that yet remained fast waning.'

The executioner – 70-year-old George Mitchell, from Somerset – waited on the drop. He quickly pulled the cap down over Weeks's face, then adjusted the noose around his neck. While the chaplain still prayed, the bolts were withdrawn and Weeks fell into eternity with a dreadful crash. His body hung lifeless, fingers still clutching a handkerchief he had carried. Some in the crowd fainted at the sight. After hanging for one hour and a minute, the body was taken down and removed inside the prison for burial.

Stone Records

Today, however, the only reminder of what took place is a monument of granite high on Roughtor, Cornwall's second highest hill, towering above Bodmin Moor. The inscription on the monument reads: 'Erected By Public Subscription In Memory Of Charlotte Dymond Who Was Murdered By Matthew Weeks, Sunday, April 14th, 1844.' The monu-

Dressed in their Sunday best, Charlotte and Weeks set out for a walk .... The girl never returned

ment stands near where Charlotte's body was found, pointing skywards like an accusing finger. Over the years, there have been many reports of 'sightings' of a girl walking the moor, dressed in a shawl and bonnet – the ghost of a girl who rests uneasily in her grave ....

Murder – Extraordinary Case

Matthew Weeks was indicted for the wilful murder of Charlotte Dimond, on the 14th of April last, by cutting her throat.

It was impossible to describe the excitement occasioned by this trial. At an early hour the court-yard was crowded with persons who appeared to have come from all parts of the county, and during the day the court was completely crammed.

Mr Cockburn, Mr Oxenham, and Mr Rowe conducted the case for the prosecution, and Mr Slade defended the prisoner.

It appeared that the prisoner and Charlotte Dimond were fellow servants in the house of a Mrs Peters, a small farmer, residing at Penhale. Charlotte Dimond was a young woman 18 years of age, an illegitimate child with 'but few friends'; but she and the prisoner had for some time kept company, as it is called in this county: the girl, however, it would seem was pleased with admiration, and was not insensible to the attention of others, and a person of the name of Prout had been favoured by her. On the morning of Sunday, the 14th of April last, Prout called at the house of Mrs Peters, and saw Charlotte, and appointed to meet her that evening at chapel. The prisoner and the deceased came down stairs together that morning. Mrs Peters asked her where she was going: she at first made no answer, but then said she should not be home at milking time, but that Matty (the prisoner) would milk her share of the cows. She and the prisoner then went away together. She was dressed in a dark green striped gown and red diamond shawl, and a dark brown silk bonnet, with light ribands, and had pattens; and she had a black silk bag, trimmed with lace, on her arm, and wore cotton gloves. The prisoner had on a dark velvet frock-coat, gray trousers, and his best boots. It was dirty, rainy weather. The prisoner came home alone, about half-past 9 o'clock in the evening; but the girl never came back again. Mrs Peters asked him where Charlotte was: he said he did not know. He then had his supper, pulled off his boots, and went to bed. The next morning Mrs Peters again asked him where Charlotte was, and he again replied he did not know. She went up into his room and found his best stockings dirty up to the garterings. She asked him how they got so dirty. He said the weather and roads were dirty. She said, 'Where is Charlotte! as you went away together, where did you go!' He said he went no further with her than Higherdown-gate, and he believed she went on the moor, and he went to a village about two miles off, and called on two families of the name of Westlake; but that they were not at home. On Tuesday Mrs Peters said, 'Matty you must know where Charlotte is, and if you don't tell me, I'll go to a magistrate before I sleep.' He then said, 'To tell you the truth, she's gone to Blissland, as Mrs Langstone has got an easier place than yours.' Mrs Peters told him it was his fault, as she had never given her any offence and she asked him how she could have got there after 4 o'clock. He said she was going to Mrs Spiers the first night. Mrs Peters said to him, 'You jealous thing: it was your work to put away the maid; and men be as plenty down there as they be at home with we.' On the Wednesday morning she again spoke to him about Charlotte, he said she had had a letter from Mrs Langstone to go to Blissland. On the Friday the butcher came there to kill a pig. The prisoner asked to be allowed to kill it. He took a knife and put it to the throat of the pig; but then he stopped, and said something had given him a turn. He then took another knife, and plunged it violently into the pig. During the week many persons had spoken to the prisoner about the girl; but he said he had parted with her at Higherdown-gate. He was then told that persons had seen him on the moor; but he said they could not swear to him as they had not spoken to him. On the Saturday evening, Mrs Peters said to him, 'Matty, what's the talk about Charlotte – I hope it is not true!' He did not speak, but went to another part of the kitchen. She then said, 'Matty, I'm quite frightened; and, if you have hurt the girl, you ought to be hanged in chains.' He made no answer; but went off to bed. The next morning (Sunday) he went out as usual to attend to the cows in his everyday dress. He saw Mrs Peters having a conversation with her son and another person, and he saw them go from home. He then went up stairs, dressed himself in his Sunday clothes, and came down stairs, having his umbrella in his hand, although it was a very fine day. Mrs Peters said to him, 'I hope you'll be back to dinner.' He said he would. He then went away, but did not return. He had been in the habit of keeping Charlotte's best clothes in his box; but a green gauze handkerchief was not with them, and therefore she must have had that with her when she went out on the Sunday, and this was found in the prisoner's velvet jacket pocket after he had left the house. Suspicion now had become very rife, and inquiries were made, and it was found that the girl had never been seen since she was in the company of the prisoner. A person of the name of Corry had seen the prisoner and a young woman in a dark dress go into the moor on the Sunday afternoon. The prisoner limped very much in his walk. He watched them for about a quarter of an hour. Richard Pethick, a farmer, who was on the moor between 7 and 6 o'clock on the Sunday afternoon, saw a man and woman coming towards the Roughter-ford. They came within 300 yards of him, and then returned and went another way. He afterwards returned and saw them again, they were 30 yards from him. He could distinguish the man's features and he limped. They appeared to be loitering: sometimes they were close together, and sometimes she walked away from him. The woman had on a dark dress. He watched them for an hour, and was sure the prisoner was the man. They were about 100 yards from Roughter-ford. A person of the name of Gard, a local preacher, was coming across the moor, and saw a man and woman loitering near the ford; they had both dark clothes on. This information having been received, foul play was more than suspected, and it was determined that the moor should be searched. Accordingly parties went out in different directions, for that purpose. They soon found some marks of pattens and the

impression of a man's shoe. They traced these a considerable way across the moor until they lost the patten marks. They, however, proceeded on their way until they came to Roughter-ford, where in a wild spot on this desolate moor, a long way from any human habitation, in an old watercourse, they found the body of the poor girl lying on its back with the throat cut in the most frightful manner, the wound extending from the back of the neck under the left ear round to the right ear. The carotid artery and windpipe were completely divided. Indeed, the head was all but cut off. A portion of the clothes was gone. There was no bonnet, shawl, pattens or shoes. Further search was then made, and about half-a-mile off, in a turf-pit, covered over, the parties found her shawl, bonnet, pattens, and shoes. It was now evident that the poor girl had come to her death by violent means; and inquiries were made about the prisoner. He had not returned; but it was found that he had called at a house many miles off on the road to Plymouth, on the Sunday when he left Mrs Peters, and he had there shown a black silk bag, which corresponded exactly with the one Charlotte Dimond had on the 14th of April. He was then traced to Plymouth, and was found walking with his brother and sister on the Hoe there. He was taken into custody; and in his pockets were found the gloves which Charlotte had worn on the last day she was seen alive. The prisoner's boots were compared with the tracks on the moor, and particularly with one adjoining the spot where the clothes were found, and they corresponded exactly. The girl's necklace was found on a bank close to the body. No blood was found on the prisoner's clothes.

On the part of the prisoner, it was urged that it was impossible but the person who committed the murder must have been covered with blood, whereas there was not any on the clothes of the prisoner.

Mr Justice PATTESON summed up in the most careful manner and with the strictest impartiality, telling the jury that it was the duty of the Judge to lay down the law, and for the jury to decide upon the facts in accordance with that law, without any consideration as to the punishment.

Reading and talking

Read through the material. If you are working in a group you may decide to read some parts aloud. You will probably have your own ideas about which aspects of the material you would like to work on and which ways of treating it particularly interest you.

The following starting points arose out of some of our thinking during the preparation of this chapter.

Justice in 1844

What facts emerge from the material about the administration of justice in 1844? e.g. Matthew Weeks was convicted and executed on *circumstantial* evidence. The execution was public.

History students in your group could be asked to research law and order in the nineteenth century in order to give you more background information.

'A time-capsule'

The writer of the magazine article suggests that from reading about the Charlotte Dymond case we can learn something of the lives of ordinary people, e.g. on March 25th (Lady Day) servants were 'hired and fired'.

Further reading of fact and fiction, including the works of Victorian novelists, will give you a fuller picture of the social history of the time and, in particular, a background to the lives of servants such as Matthew and Charlotte.

Fact or opinion?

Look closely at the material. Make lists of:
- what you consider to be the *facts* in the case.
- what is reported as if it is *fact* and what is obviously *gossip* and *opinion*.

Discuss your findings.

Form

Focus on the discovery of the body which is reported in both the *Times* newspaper and the magazine article.
- What do you notice about the differences in style between the two accounts?
- Suggest reasons why they are so different.
- What conclusions do you come to about the kinds of readership for whom each article was intended?

Writing

Write an account of the murder as it might appear in a 'popular' newspaper today.

Imagine that you were living at the time when the tragedy occurred. Give yourself a name and a background; you may choose to be one of the people mentioned in the articles.

Select one of the following forms of writing in order to express your point of view about the murder. In each case decide who your audience is.
- Letter
- Diary
- Interview
- Sermon

Work sharing

Share some of your work through well-prepared readings or by acting out the situation described, e.g. sermon.

Select some examples of each form for possible re-drafting, typing and reproducing.

You may want to use some of this work as part of a Documentary Drama.

'The Murder of Charlotte Dymond'

The following extracts are taken from a book by Pat Munn, a Cornish historian. An enquiry from the author, Colin Wilson, who was collecting material for a series of articles on jealousy murders, led Pat Munn to discover the original brief to the prosecuting council. She subsequently spent five years in painstaking research.

In her fascinating and very readable book, Pat Munn makes a powerful case for believing that Matthew Weeks' original statement to the constable (set out below) was, in fact, the truth.

In the morning (of Sunday, April 14), Charlotte told me that her mistress (Mrs Peter) had given her a week's warning (notice) and that she was going to leave; and she asked me to lend her half-a-crown. I let her have 18 pence and asked where she was going. She said she did not know. Then she asked me if I would go along with her a little way in the afternoon. I went along with her a little way the other side of the (Altarnon-Camelford) road going to chapel; and then she said she did not want me to go any further, I wished her well and bid her good afternoon, and she left me and I left her. I did not speak to her any more. The blood on the shirt was when the pig was killed.

Now here are the letter and the confession which Matthew Weeks is said to have dictated during his stay in Bodmin gaol.

The letter is interesting in that it tells us some details about Matthew's belongings and his wishes concerning their disposal. It reads like a will.

The Letter
My dear father and mother, and dear brothers and sisters, and uncles and aunts, and I hope my dear brothers and sisters will now take a warning by me. My brothers will not place too much confidence in young maidens; and my sisters not in young men. And I hope that my brother John that he will make a great alteration upon this; and I hope he will seek the Lord because he might be cut off to a minute's notice, and he will not have time to, I hope that he will knock up drinking and attend to a place of worship, and not break the sabbath so much as he has; and William too, and pray think on this when you don't see me.

You may ask the blacksmith, John Doney, what I owe him and I wish you to pay it little or much. I give my love to Maria Doney and Susan, Maria and Thomasine Hayne, and bid them all farewell. If my brother Richard will call at the gaol any time, he will have my hat, braces and stock and half-shirt; and he must please to give the £5 to mother. The clothes box at Mrs Peter's, I give to mother. There are two watch ribbons in my box; give the one with a seal to it to William and the other to John, to keep for my sake. Mother must have the shirts and stockings. There are two hats. Give one to William and the other to John; and two pairs of trousers and a pair of leggings which mother can do as shee please with; also a fustian jacket, three waistcoats and two handkerchiefs.

Bennett, the constable, has an umbrella, a pair of trousers, drawers and a round jacket, and a black silk handkerchief for mother to do as she please with. He has got a watch, which please to give to brother John. There is a horn cable to a threshell at Mrs Peter's which I should like mother to have again. Mr Everest (the governor) has been a very kind friend to me since I have been here, and Mr Kendall (the chaplain) too. Dingle, the constable, have got my velvet jacket and a pair of boots which mother must have and do as she please with. I wish all my brothers and sisters all farewell and all my friends.

I am your unfortunate son,
X (the sign of Matthew Weeks)

The confession
On Sunday afternoon, the 14th April, Charlotte Dymond went out of Mrs Peter's house, at Penhale in the parish of Davidstow, about half-past four. I saw her go and very shortly afterwards followed her. When I overtook her, I asked her where she was going; she said for a walk. We then strolled on together towards the moors. Our conversation for a long time was on indifferent subjects. Towards dusk, we had some words together about her giving her company to some other young men, and our words became more high when I told her that I had seen her in a situation with some young man that was disgraceful to her.

She then said 'I shall do as I like, I shall have nothing more to say to you.' This expression aroused my anger so much that I took out my knife and went towards her to commit the bloody deed. Something came across me and I shut the knife and put it into my pocket. On her repeating the words 'I shall do as I like, I shall have nothing more to say to you,' I again took my knife out of my pocket, approached behind her and made a cut at her throat while she was standing. She never saw me take the knife out, nor was she aware of what I was going to do.

She immediately fell backwards, the blood gushing out in a large stream and exclaimed whilst falling 'Lord have mercy upon me'. When she was on the ground, I made a second and much larger cut, though she was almost dead at the time. The only way I can account for so little blood being on the spot is that it must have run into the little stream that lay close by the spot where I committed the awful deed.

After standing over her body about four or five minutes, I lifted up one of her arms and it fell to the ground as if she was dead. I then pushed her body a little further down the bank. I afterwards took her bonnet, shawl, shoes and pattens and covered them up in a turf pit. Her gloves and bag, I put into my pocket and then went towards home, and in my road I threw away the knife, which I hope no-one will ever find, as I never wish the instrument to be seen with which I committed the deed.

The bag I also threw away in my road to Plymouth. I never thought of murdering Charlotte Dymond till a few minutes before I cut her throat.

The alleged confession by Matthew Weeks is one of the pieces of evidence which Pat Munn uses to demolish the prosecution case against him. The important factors are:
1 She points to a discrepancy between the claim by Weeks that he saw Charlotte leave Penhale at 4.30 p.m. and the witnesses for the prosecution who stated that they left together at 4 p.m.
2 The knife described by Matthew was obviously a common pocket knife, the only one he had, and could not have been the weapon used to inflict the violent injuries described.
3 If Charlotte fell backwards as he suggests, with 'the blood gushing out in a large stream', it is difficult to explain why he was not covered in blood.

Debating

Having read all the evidence, does there now exist in your mind a reasonable doubt about Matthew Weeks' guilt? How say you?

Debate the motion that 'This house believes that Matthew Weeks was wrongly convicted of the murder of Charlotte Dymond'.

Ballad form

The word 'ballad' comes from the Latin *ballare*, meaning 'to dance'. Ballads are among the earliest forms of oral narrative poetry often supported by music and dance. Features common to both traditional and modern ballads are:
- four line stanzas (quatrains);
- regular metre and rhyme;
- economy of language; and
- a vivid story line, often concerned with violent events and themes involving jealousy and revenge.

It is not surprising that such a sensational story as the Charlotte Dymond case should have captured the imagination of the Cornish poet, Charles Causley.

The Ballad of Charlotte Dymond

It was a Sunday evening
   And in the April rain
That Charlotte went from our house
   And never came home again.

Her shawl of diamond redcloth,
　　She wore a yellow gown,
She carried the green gauze handkerchief
　　She bought in Bodmin town.

About her throat her necklace
　　And in her purse her pay:
The four silver shillings
　　She had at Lady Day.

In her purse four shillings
　　And in her purse her pride
As she walked out one evening
　　Her lover at her side.

Out beyond the marshes
　　Where the cattle stand,
With her crippled lover
　　Limping at her hand.

Charlotte walked with Matthew
　　Through the Sunday mist,
Never saw the razor
　　Waiting at his wrist.

Charlotte she was gentle
　　But they found her in the flood
Her Sunday beads among the reeds
　　Beaming with her blood.

Matthew, where is Charlotte,
　　And wherefore has she flown?
For you walked out together
　　And now are come alone.

Why do you not answer,
　　Stand silent as a tree,
Your Sunday worsted stockings
　　All muddied to the knee?

Why do you mend your breast-pleat
　　With a rusty needle's thread
And fall with fears and silent tears
　　Upon your single bed?

Why do you sit so sadly
　　Your face the colour of clay
And with a green gauze handkerchief
　　Wipe the sour sweat away?

Has she gone to Blisland
    To seek an easier place,
And is that why your eye won't dry
    And blinds your bleaching face?

'Take me home!' cried Charlotte,
    'I lie here in the pit!
A red rock rests upon my breasts
    And my naked neck is split!'

Her skin was soft as sable,
    Her eyes were wide as day,
Her hair was blacker than the bog
    That licked her life away.

Her cheeks were made of honey,
    Her throat was made of flame
Where all around the razor
    Had written its red name.

As Matthew turned at Plymouth
    About the tilting Hoe,
The cold and cunning Constable
    Up to him did go:

'I've come to take you, Matthew,
    Unto the Magistrate's door.
Come quiet now, you pretty poor boy,
    And you must know what for.'

'She is as pure,' cried Matthew,
    'As is the early dew,
Her only stain it is the pain
    That round her neck I drew!

'She is as guiltless as the day
    She sprang forth from her mother.
The only sin upon her skin
    Is that she loved another.'

They took him off to Bodmin,
    They pulled the prison bell,
They sent him smartly up to Heaven
    And dropped him down to Hell.

All through the granite kingdom
    And on its travelling airs
Ask which of these two lovers
    The most deserves your prayers.

And your steel heart search, Stranger,
   That you may pause and pray
For lovers who come not to bed
   Upon their wedding day,

But lie upon the moorland
   Where stands the sacred snow
Above the breathing river,
   And the salt sea-winds go.

When the poem was set to music, a minor key was chosen to
match the mood and meaning of the words. The ballad is long,
so the pace of the song must keep moving onwards. Perhaps
alternate groups of verses could be spoken to the
accompaniment of humming, tuned instruments and percussion.

163

This arrangement is to be thought of as a base on which to structure any modifications, ideas and talents you may have within your group. A suggested guitar accompaniment would be simple arpeggios in the chords as marked.

Reading

Experiment with various ways of reading the ballad. Try not to let the rhyme and rhythm take over the meaning and cancel out the feeling!

Use the guitar accompaniment provided in the ways suggested.

Talking

What details and events are included and highlighted in the ballad in order to make a vivid, dramatic statement?

Writing

In the eighteenth and nineteenth centuries, ballads claiming to be the words of a confessing convict were very popular.

Write a ballad called 'The True Confession of Matthew Weeks'.

Documentary drama

The making of your own documentary programme based on this story, presents you with the opportunity to draw upon:
- the literary stimulus material in this chapter;
- your own research;
- creative work in writing, art and music;
- drama skills.

Writing and drawing

We have provided you with an ideas page opposite. You may like to produce one of your own or select from ours.

The selection of ideas and form of presentation will depend upon your preferences, expertise and the resources available.

Do not be too ambitious; aim for simplicity, effectiveness and practicability in your organisation of the material.

Selection and organisation

Choose a starting point under which to group associated ideas. As you can see, we have blocked ours inside the Roughtor Stone.

Presentation

If you decide to share your work with an invited audience, (it could be the third years), you will need to:
- plan your 'set' with the 'audience' in mind;
- rehearse your drama;
- make use of lighting, sound effects and costume.

Post script

Here are some ideas for talk, writing and drama, as expressed by fourth year students who chose to set their own assignments.

Talking

- From the evidence available, could any other person have murdered Charlotte?
- How far did local hostility and prejudice influence the jury?
- Why did the *Times* article report the pig killing incident?
- What are your views on capital punishment?

Starting Point: a back projection of Roughtor Monument.

Scenes:

1 A group of students with notebooks; guide tells murder story ending with true stories of recent sightings of a woman on the moor 'who was wearing a gown of different colours, a red cloth shawl and bonnet of silk. She kept stopping and shading her eyes from the sun, as if looking for someone'.

2 The ghost of Charlotte Dymond moves us back in time to 1844, accompanied by the first three verses of the ballad, said or sung.

3 Voices from the past to include gossip between villagers; the arrest; the statement; witnesses at the trial; summing up; confession. (Mixture of original source material and creative writing.)

4 Last three verses of ballad, said or sung. Charlotte's 'ghost' returns to the stone.

5 Students disperse discussing the recent sightings of the ghost and the implications. Why is Charlotte's spirit not at rest?

Writing

- Write a letter as the solicitor of Weeks, appealing for a new trial. Give facts of bias which must have influenced the jury.
- Write an account of the events of the 14th April, 1844 as if you were Matthew Weeks dictating to another person.
- Write a letter from the ghost of Charlotte Dymond.

Drama

- Act out the scene in which Matthew Weeks' family receive his final letter.
- This scene takes place in a public house in Bodmin. Villagers are talking about the murder and the trial. Some people think Weeks was guilty; others insist that he could have been innocent.
- Act out the trial of Matthew Weeks.

8 Focus on a theme

Run for Cover

The previous chapter was primarily concerned with exploring ways of working with fact and fiction, not with the theme of 'murder'. This chapter, by contrast, starts with the theme, 'Run for Cover', and asks you to suggest the range of possible forms in which to explore it.

In order to focus on a theme through an exciting, creative and reflective approach, you need to:
- think big!;
- brainstorm in groups;
- focus on *one* idea;
- select ideas for further development;
- start talking, reading, writing and improvising as you collect your material;
- organise your work into an appropriate form, e.g. anthology, school assembly, examination course work, practical drama examination, sharing with an invited audience, a series of drawings or paintings, sculpture.

Here is one example for you to work with:

Stage One – Think Big

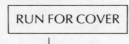

RUN FOR COVER
↓

Stage Two – Brainstorm
↓

Hide and Seek
Homes
Institutions – hospitals, prisons
Masks and Disguises
Running Away from Oneself
Slogan for Insurance Company
Hiding behind Authority
Disasters – Famine, Flood, War

Stage Three – Select One Area
↓

WAR

↓

Stage Four

Focus on one aspect
Collect material

We chose to collect material in which writers remember individuals 'running for cover' in wartime situations.

VALERIE AVERY

A Wartime Childhood

The days were short then. Often we slept during the day and kept awake all night ready to go when the air-raid warden got the signal through on his crackling relay wireless. Usually he warned us in good time, so that we could be settled in the shelter long before the 'warning' sounded. He had one leg shorter than the other, which was why he couldn't fight abroad, Mum told me. You could hear him coming along dragging his foot – drag-step-drag-step. There was no need for him to come down to the basement, for as soon as we heard old Siren Step we began to look for the candles. Mum said that I would have a leg like that if I didn't eat my greens or, worse still, she said that I wouldn't grow at all, like the man who sold newspapers on the corner. His face was old and wrinkled, he looked about sixty, but he was only as tall as Tommy.

Sometimes Siren Step was too late and we had to get out of the bath quick and go running down to the shelter dripping wet and naked.

We were always waiting for sounds, especially the siren. When the 'warning' sounded we all rushed to the shelter at the bottom of the garden. Mum was the last to come in, clutching her insurance policies in one hand, candles and matches in the other. The shelter smelt of earth, candle grease and Ibcol, which Mum splashed down every day to ward away earwigs and spiders, but they still crawled over our four bunks; Mum and I slept on one; Tommy and Arf on another; Ann, baby Anny and Piggy Boo on another; and the fourth bunk was used by Ann's sister, Emma, whose husband was away fighting.

We sat in the damp, dark shelter wrapped in blankets, sipping warm, watery cocoa, sometimes for the whole night. Sometimes it was so quiet as we waited and waited that you could hear the grease trickling down to its holder. Often Mum read us stories and the giants she was reading about appeared on the walls as the candle flame danced in the draught. Emma tried to knit but she kept stopping to pick up dropped stitches. Nobody knew what she was making, it never seemed to grow. Ann's face was white and taut, her mouth kept twitching. When Piggy Boo started to cry she unbuttoned her cardigan and cradled her in her arms, rocking backwards and forwards.

'There, there. That's better.' Everyone whispered down in the shelter, even Ann. 'Now don't you bite too hard.'

Sleeping was difficult. Tommy and Arf fought for room, tried to push one another out of the bunk and then voices were raised.

'Stop it, you two. You'll wake the babies, and it takes long enough to get 'em off. What's the ma'er with you, Arf? You're old enough now to be a bit patient . . . .'

' . . . But 'e takes up all the room. Tell 'im to move over.'

'Blast! I've dropped another stitch. Do as your mother tells you.'

'It's 'im, Aunt 'Em. I get blamed for everythink round 'ere. You wait till I get you outside, Tommy. I'm gonna break . . .'

' . . . Wait till your father comes 'ome, then we'll see 'oo's gonna do the breakin'. Come on, Di, bring up windy,' and she rubbed the baby's back.

All the time the siren surpassed these human sounds. When it stopped everything else stopped. We strained our ears for the far-away sound of the 'doodle bugs'. Soon in the distance the dreadful droning was heard, coming nearer and nearer, getting louder and louder. Now passing over the shelter vibrating all around, bursting our eardrums. The women hugged us closer. They kissed us and we felt their nerve-tight limbs, their dry lips and their hearts beating urgently. They tried to sing bits of hymns, their voices echoing like ghosts in the empty shell of the shelter. Then they stopped and we heard silence. We heard our hearts beating, even baby Anny's. We were all waiting for the next sound. Silence became a feeling; the women waiting for that bomb to drop, we children waiting for them to release their biting grip on our flesh, waiting for them to breathe 'Amen' to the silent prayer their lips quivered.

'Jesus Christ save us!' The bomb earthquaked all around and we were thrown into a heap. We lay there in the darkness not daring to move until the 'all clear' sounded. Then the candles were re-lit, the babies started crying, the boys fought to get out of the shelter and the women knelt.

'Thank you, Christ, for saving us this night. Now for a fag.'

NORMAN NICHOLSON

The Evacuees

Four years ago
They came to this little town[1]
Carrying their bundles – women who did not know
Where the sky would lie when their babies were born, mothers
With children, children with sisters and brothers,
Children with schoolmates, and frightened children alone.
They saw the strangers at the station, the sea-mist on the hill,
In the windless waiting days when the walls of Poland fell.[2]

Winter came
And the wind did not rise; the sky
Withheld its threat of thunderbolt or bomb.
The women were lonely. Thoughts began to bend
To Northumbrian voices high as a seagull's cry,
To the smell of the North Sea in the streets, the foggy air,
The fish-shops and the neighbours. The tide of fear
Flowed back, leaving weary empty sand.

The women returned
To the Tyneside husbands and the Tyneside coal,
And most of the children followed. Others stayed and learned
The Cumberland vowels, took strangers for their friends,
Went home for holidays at first, then not at all,
Accepted in the aisle the bishop's hands,
Won scholarships and badges, and were known
One with the indigenous children of the town.

Four years ago
They came, and in four childhood years
The memory shrivels and the muscles grow.
The little girl who wept on the platform then
Now feels her body blossom like the trees,
Discovers tennis, poetry and flowers,
And under the dripping larches in the rain
Knows the first experiment of a kiss.

Will they rest,
Will they be contented, these
Fledglings of a cuckoo's egg reared in a stranger's nest?
Born of one people, with another bred,
Will they return to their parents again, or choose
The foster-home, or seek the unrented road?
Grant that in the future they may find
A rock on which to build a house for heart and mind.

---

[1] Millom, on the west coast of Cumberland where Norman Nicholson was born and still lives.

[2] The German invasion of Poland in August 1939 led to Britain's declaration of war.

VERNON SCANNELL

Gunpowder Plot

For days these curious cardboard buds have lain
In brightly coloured boxes. Soon the night
Will come. We pray there'll be no rain
To make these magic orchids flame less bright.

Now in the garden's darkness they begin
To flower: the frenzied whizz of Catherine-wheel
Puts forth its fiery petals and the thin
Rocket soars to burst upon the steel

Bulwark of a cloud. And then the guy,
Absurdly human phoenix, is again
Gulped by greedy flames: the harvest sky
Is flecked with threshed and gòlden grain.

'Uncle! A cannon! Watch me as I light it!'
The women, helter-skelter, squealing high,
Retreat; the paper fuse is quickly lit,
A cat-like hiss and spit of fire, a sly

Falter, then the air is shocked with blast
The cannon bangs, and in my nostrils drifts
A bitter scent that brings the lurking past
Lurching to my side. The present shifts,

Allows a ten-year memory to walk
Unhindered now; and so I'm forced to hear
The banshee howl of mortar and the talk
Of men who died; am forced to taste my fear.

I listen for a moment to the guns,
The torn earth's grunts, recalling how I prayed.
The past retreats. I hear a corpse's sons:
'Who's scared of bangers?' 'Uncle! John's afraid!'

SIEGFRIED SASSOON

The Hero

'Jack fell as he'd have wished,' the Mother said,
And folded up the letter that she'd read.
'The Colonel writes so nicely.' Something broke
In the tired voice that quavered to a choke.
She half looked up. 'We mothers are so proud
Of our dead soldiers.' Then her face was bowed.

Quietly the Brother Officer went out.
He'd told the poor old dear some gallant lies
That she would nourish all her days, no doubt.
For while he coughed and mumbled, her weak eyes
Had shone with gentle triumph, brimmed with joy,
Because he'd been so brave, her glorious boy.

He thought how 'Jack', cold-footed, useless swine,
Had panicked down the trench that night the mine
Went up at Wicked Corner; how he'd tried
To get sent home, and how, at last, he died,
Blown to small bits. And no one seemed to care
Except that lonely woman with white hair.

WILLIS HALL

from: The Long And The Short And The Tall

BAMFORTH   So we share out what we've got.
MITCHEM   No.
BAMFORTH   He gets half of mine.
MITCHEM   No! There's none for him.
BAMFORTH   He'll have to have a drink sometime. He can't go the distance without – you've got to get him back as well. [*He waits for a reply.*] We're taking him as well!
MITCHEM   I'm sorry.
JOHNSTONE   He's stopping where he is. [*He picks up* THE PRISONER*'s bayonet from the table.*] It's cobbler's for him.
BAMFORTH   No.
MITCHEM   I've got no choice.
BAMFORTH   You said he was going back.
MITCHEM   He was – before. The circumstances are altered. The situation's changed. I can't take him along.
BAMFORTH   What's the poor get done to us?
MITCHEM   It's a war. It's something in a uniform and it's a different shade to mine.
BAMFORTH   [*positioning himself between* THE PRISONER *and* JOHNSTONE]   You're not doing it, Johnno.
JOHNSTONE   You laying odds on that?
BAMFORTH   For Christ's sake!
JOHNSTONE   It's a bloody Nip.
BAMFORTH   He's a man!
JOHNSTONE (*crossing a few paces towards* THE PRISONER)   Shift yourself, Bamforth. Get out of the way.
BAMFORTH   You're not doing it.
MITCHEM   Bamforth, shift yourself.
BAMFORTH   You're a bastard, Mitchem.
MITCHEM   I wish to God I was.
BAMFORTH   You're a dirty bastard, Mitchem.
MITCHEM   As far as I'm concerned, it's all these lads or him.
BAMFORTH   It's him and me.
MITCHEM [*crossing to join* JOHNSTONE]   Get to one side. That's an order.

BAMFORTH   Stick it.

MITCHEM   For the last time, Bamforth, move over.

BAMFORTH   Try moving me.

MITCHEM   I've not got time to mess about.

BAMFORTH   So come on, Whitaker! Don't sit there, lad. Whose side you on? [WHITAKER *rises slowly from the form. For a moment it would seem that he is going to stand by* BAMFORTH *but he crosses the room to stand beyond* MITCHEM *and* JOHNSTONE] You've got no guts, Whitaker. You know that, boy? You've just got no guts.

WHITAKER   We've got to get back, Bammo.

BAMFORTH   You're a gutless slob!

WHITAKER   I've got to get back!

BAMFORTH   Evans. Taffy, Taff! [EVANS *turns from the window*] Put the gun on these two, son.

EVANS   I reckon Mitch is right, you know. We couldn't get him back to camp, could we, boyo? The Nips must have a Div between the camp and us.

BAMFORTH   He's going to kill him, you nit!

EVANS   You never know about that fag case, do you, son?

BAMFORTH   What's the fag case got to do with it! . . . Smudger! Smudger, now it's up to you.

SMITH   Don't ask me, Bammo. Leave me out of it.

BAMFORTH   You're in it, Smudge. You're in it up to here.

SMITH   I just take orders. I just do as I'm told. I just plod on.

BAMFORTH   The plodding on has stopped. Right here. Right here you stop and make a stand. He's got a wife and kids.

SMITH   I've got a wife and kids myself. Drop it, Bammo, it's like Mitch says – it's him·or us.

BAMFORTH   Jock! . . . Jock! [MACLEISH *continues to stare out of the window.*] Macleish! . . . [MACLEISH *does not move.*] I hope they carve your brother up. Get that? I hope they carve your bloody brother up!

MITCHEM   All right, Bamforth, you've had your say. Now shift.

BAMFORTH   Shift me! Come on, heroes, shift me!

MITCHEM   Whitaker! Grab a gun and cover the Nip.

BAMFORTH   Don't do it, Whitaker. Stay out of it.

MITCHEM   Whitaker!

[WHITAKER *picks up a sten from the table and crosses to cover* THE PRISONER, *who has realized the implications and is trembling with fear.* MITCHEM *and* JOHNSTONE *move forward to overpower* BAMFORTH. JOHNSTONE *drops the bayonet on the floor and, together with* MITCHEM, *grapples with* BAMFORTH. *As they fight* THE PRISONER *begins to rise to his feet.*]

WHITAKER   [*already in a state of fear himself*]: Get down! . . . Sit down! . . . [THE PRISONER *continues to rise.*] Sit down, you stupid man, or I'll have to put a bullet into you . . . [THE PRISONER *is standing upright as* WHITAKER'*s finger tightens on the trigger. A long burst from the sten shudders the hut and the bullets slam home into the body of* THE PRISONER *like hammer blows.* THE PRISONER *doubles up and falls to the floor. The fight stops. There is a pause.* WHITAKER *drops the sten and buries his face in his hands.*] God . . . God . . . God . . . [*His voice swells.*] Oh, God!

DAVID BOULTON

from: The Conchies

In this extract from his book *Objection Overruled*, David Boulton, the young English T.V. writer, tells of the men who, in the First World War, rebelled against being conscripted into the Army.

'Pasty-faces' they were called at first. Then the soldiers dubbed them 'conchies,' which caught on rather better. *The Times* called them pacifists until Northcliffe forbade his editor to print the word, sternly warning that 'advertising pacifism is the way to promote it.'

The British public, grimly preoccupied by the horrors of an apparently unending war which was producing a 'wastage' of one in every six soldiers dispatched to the front, became abruptly aware of conscientious objectors when, in the spring and summer of 1916, more than 1,000 of them led the first open, defiant resistance to conscription – introduced to Britain that year. They were organised and supported by the No-Conscription Fellowship, founded by Fenner Brockway.

Altogether, according to statistics compiled at the end of the war by the N-CF Records Department, 6,261 men resisted the Military Service Acts. They were arrested and handed over to the Army. Those who continued their resistance by refusing to obey orders numbered 5,739. All were court-martialled, 655 of them twice, 521 three times, 319 four times, 50 five times and three six times. The N-CF's leaders, including Fenner Brockway, Clifford Allen and Bertrand Russell, went to jail. Its weekly newspaper, *The Tribunal*, was suppressed and its printing plant seized by the police.

As a direct result of the treatment they were accorded in military and civil prisons, 39 were driven insane and 71 objectors died either while undergoing punishment or immediately after a hastily contrived release on medical grounds.

The Army devised its own means of bringing the rebels to heel. Legally the objectors were soldiers of the King. Soldiers could be posted overseas. Disobedience at the front was punishable by death at the hands of a firing-squad. So the War Office reached for its ultimate deterrent, and in its determination to make the deterrent credible clashed dramatically with the civil authorities to whom it was theoretically responsible.

*

One now-forgotten scandal concerned a young solicitor's clerk from Manchester, James Brightmore. For refusing to be put under military orders Brightmore was sentenced at Shore Camp, Cleethorpes, to 28 days' detention in solitary confinement. But there was no unoccupied cell in the guardroom, so the major in charge commanded that a pit be dug in the open. It measured three feet by two at the surface, and tapered off to two feet six inches by 15 inches at a depth of 12 feet. The pit became

Brightmore's cell.

When it began to fill with water, two strips of wood were fixed just above the water line for him to stand on. This was described as 'favoured treatment'. His comrades, said the guards, had been sent to France for execution at the front. He would be sent there, too, if he refused to co-operate. He did refuse. After eight days a sympathetic soldier smuggled into the pit a cigarette packet and a stub of pencil, and Brightmore wrote a half-demented note to his family on the back of the packet. 'The sun beats down, and through the long day there are only the walls of clay to look at. Already I am half-mad. What have our friends been doing?'

Brightmore's family sent the note to the *Manchester Guardian*, which commented on it. Forty minutes after the paper arrived at the camp Brightmore was removed from the pit to the guardroom, after 11 days' confinement. The pit was hastily filled in, but too late for concealment. The Major responsible was court-martialled and dismissed.

Cases such as these, combined with the fact that the N-CF was boasting of having formed branches in Army units and guardrooms, forced the Government in July, 1916, to end the procedure whereby objectors were handed over to the Army. Instead, they were committed either to civil prisons or to special Home Office work camps.

The first Home Office settlement was at the remote village of Dyce, near Aberdeen. Nearly 250 men were quartered in tents which had been condemned as unfit for soldiers in France but nevertheless seemed to the authorities adequate for conscientious objectors.

The tents were pitched in a permanent sea of mud. The men, already worn down by months of Army brutality, imprisonment and under-feeding, were set to heavy work in granite quarries. Walter Roberts, a 20-year-old from Stockport, collapsed with a high fever. He was refused medical attention, or removal to the village quarters occupied by settlement staff. For five days he was nursed by his friends, first in a stable and then in a disused cottage. On the fifth day he died. A few days later Dyce was abruptly closed. But 70 more C.O.s died before the war ended.

*

The 'pasty-faces' lost their battles – for the repeal of conscription and for absolute exemption on grounds of conscience – but they won their war. They struck their special blow for liberty, and helped to create 50 years ago a climate more liberal than exists today in many democratic countries, including the U.S.A. Among all the other anniversaries of World War I which have been so widely commemorated, the anniversary of this fight against war surely deserves its place

Working for the war effort: woman loading coke at the South
Metropolitan Gas Works, Old Kent Road, London

BELGRADE THEATRE IN EDUCATION

from: Killed: July 17th 1916

[BILLY *lights a candle and starts to write.*]

[*Lights up on* MAY *in the munitions factory.*]

MAY [*writing*] July 16th, 7 o'clock.
   [*She reads through her letter while putting on her hat.*]
   My darling Billy, hoping you are well as I am. I thought I'd
   start this little note now and try and get it finished in me
   breaks. I'm doing a night shift tonight.
   [ELSIE *enters. She hangs up her shawl and starts to put on her overall.*]
   But don't worry, Elsie's here to look after me.

ELSIE Not another letter. That poor boy must be up to his ears in
   them by now, the number you send.

MAY [*still writing*] He likes them. Oh my God, is it time?

ELSIE Mmm.

MAY Right, I'll have to finish this later now.
[*They start work.*]
Oh my God, Elsie, I'm that tired. I hardly got any sleep today. Bloomin' kids were out in the street playing tin-tan-alley-man at the tops of their voices.

ELSIE Mother was trying to keep my lot quiet. Fat chance.

MAY Is she looking after them tonight? Is she?

ELSIE No, George.

MAY Oh eh, he's getting his feet under the mat, isn't he? Be moving in next!

ELSIE Don't be so wet. He's very good with them. The boys love him, especially Sammy. Thinks the world of him. Makes him into a real hero.

MAY Oh. It'll be a shame when he has to go. Has he had his call-up papers yet?

ELSIE Yes, they came last week.

MAY Oh, Charlie Harris had his last week and he's got to go on Monday and he's got a hacking cough. Me dad says they'll be taking them with wooden legs next.

ELSIE They're taking anything now. And he's married, Charlie Harris. It's hitting families hard now they're forcing men to go.

MAY Aye, well, they need them. They need all the men they can get.

ELSIE I remember when this factory was full of men. Now look at it. Three left. That's why they've got us here. 'Cos there aren't any men left. We're filling up dead men's places here.

MAY Don't be so morbid. They're not all dead.

ELSIE Did you see that man in the pub the other night? Sitting over in the corner. His hand was shaking so he couldn't hold his beer glass. He looked dreadful. Shell shock, that's what they're calling it. He'd no control. His nerves were all shot to pieces. He'll never work again, that feller.

MAY I know, poor man. My God, these bullets. D'you know I dream about them?

ELSIE Do you? So do I.

MAY Yeah.

ELSIE I'm packing bullets in me sleep now.

MAY D'you know Elsie, no kidding, the other day I woke up and I was saying 'More bullets, more bullets, more bullets.'
[ELSIE *laughs.*]

ELSIE I wonder how many we've made since we've been working here.

MAY [*unthoughtfully*] Thousands.
[*They continue to work.*]
So when's George going, then?

ELSIE He won't be going.

MAY Why, is something wrong with him?

ELSIE No, there's nothing wrong with him.

MAY Well why isn't he going, then?

ELSIE He says he's not going. He's sent back his papers. He's refusing to go. He says nobody's got the right to make his decisions for him.

MAY   Well, it's the same for everybody else.

ELSIE   He says nobody's got the right to tell him to kill men he doesn't want to kill, if it's against his conscience.

MAY   Oh, he's a conchie, then.

ELSIE   That's what they call them.

MAY   Don't you mind?

ELSIE   He's a good man, May.

MAY   People will say he's a coward.

ELSIE   Well, people can say what they like.

[*Lights fade.*]

[*Lights up in a different area.*]

R.S.M.   Fall in. You've all heard the sentence passed by Field General Court Martial – Private Dean is to be shot by firing squad at dawn tomorrow. This sentence has been confirmed by the Commander-in-Chief Field Marshall Sir Douglas Haig. The Officer in charge of the execution is Captain Howard. He has picked ten names at random from the remaining soldiers in this battalion: Prowse, Wood, Bromelow, Walsh, Green, Stirling. You six men will form the firing squad. You will hand your rifles in to me, cleaned and in good working order. At dawn tomorrow you will be handed your rifles back, each with a single round of ammunition, five rounds will be live, the sixth blank. You all know the reason for this. Walsh!

WALSH   [*off*] Sir!

R.S.M.   You will accompany me to the hut and escort the prisoner to the place of execution.

WALSH   [*off*] Sir.

R.S.M.   The remaining four names: Dunn, Faulkes, Sudlow, Nelson – you will act as stretcher-bearers and remove the corpse after the execution, and take it on a limber to a place of burial. You will be informed of the exact whereabouts later. The prisoner is locked up on the other side of the farmyard. You will be billeted in this hut. You can brew tea here and eat your rations. The owner of this farm and his daughter know what's going on. If any of you men come into contact with these people you will say nothing – is that clear?

WALSH   [*off*] Permission to speak, Sir.

R.S.M.   What is it?

WALSH   [*off*] What's he doing?

R.S.M.   Writing a letter. Any more questions? Right, fall out!

[*The* R.S.M. *leaves.* WALSH *enters and moves into the light.*]

WALSH   Walsh, you will accompany me to the hut and escort the prisoner to the place of execution.

We're going to shoot Bill Dean tomorrow just because he got lost. I wonder what they'd do if we all got lost . . . . All the corporals, all the sergeants, all the generals – if the whole army got lost. I wonder what the Sergeant Major would say. 'Sorry we're late, Sir, but we got lost. Oh no, Sir, not just me, the whole army got lost. What's that, Sir? We're all going to be shot? If the whole army's going to be shot, Sir, who's going to shoot us? [*Pause.*] Oh, I see, Sir, we've all got to shoot ourselves. Sorry I was late. Bang!' – the Sergeant would.

I could be home by now, doing me garden, planting turnips. Nice row of turnips there, nice row of peas there, ivy on that back wall. No! runner beans, just below 'em potatoes. After all that hard work, down the road for a pint. 'Evening George, pint please, oh, nice head on it. Well, Cheers! What's that George? Oh, we're growing leeks in the trenches now, roses round the dugout, I'm using my tin helmet as a hanging basket . . . celery in the shell holes, sweet peas on the barbed wire. Oh yes, it's very nice. The Germans? No, they mostly grow crocuses.'

I wonder if the Sergeant Major's got a garden? He's probably concreted it. We could all lay down our rifles tomorrow. 'Here you are, Sir. We don't feel right about shooting Bill Dean, we're all going home. No, not just me, all of us. I'm going home to see my Missus. Well, cheerio! Bye for now and all that. Don't forget to write.' They'd shoot us. They'd shoot us . . .

[*Pause.*]

'I don't think I should be on this firing squad, Sir . . . I know his family. I know his family.'

[*Lights fade on* WALSH.]

PENELOPE LIVELY

from: *Going Back*

Mike was a conchie. 'A what?' said Edward, fork half-way to mouth, and for once we attend to an explanation, because, somehow, we feel involved.

'A conscientious objector,' said Betty. 'And don't think you're leaving that corned beef, Edward, because you're not. That's someone that doesn't believe in fighting so they're not called up but they've got to do war work. Go down the mines or on the land.'

And the status provoked discussion. People had opinions, it seemed, about conchies.

'I dunno,' said Susie, 'I think they should have to join up. I mean, if everyone felt like that . . .'

'There'd be no wars, would there?' said Betty tartly.

'I mean, our soldiers are fighting for them too, aren't they, whether they want people fighting for them or not.'

'It's their religion, isn't it, some of them?'

'Bolshies,' said Sandy darkly.

'It's not how I'd see things,' said Betty, 'not with Hitler. But everyone's entitled to their opinion.'

'They gave them white feathers, last time,' said Sandy, 'the women did. For cowardice, see.'

*

Mike was twenty. We had married him, in our minds, to Susie, but Susie was twenty-three, which made Mike no good to her at all, not when there were soldiers on Treborough Common. So Pam and Susie teased Mike and Mike grinned and didn't care and Betty piled food high on his plate because he was too thin. And even Sandy, who knew what he felt about conchies, said he was a nice enough lad, one way and another, when all was said and done.

Mike found the violin in the attic.

'Good Lord,' he said. 'It works.' And he held the thing under his chin, like people in pictures, and capered about with it, carving lush and wild sounds and leaning over us, singing into our ears, a soaring song like the Italian prisoners sang up on Croydon Hill. I had never heard anything so funny – I hugged myself with delight, begged him to go on. But Edward was not amused. He had gone all intense, like a dog pointing.

'How do you know how to do it? How does it work? Show me.'

And Mike, amiable, showed. 'Right. Hand round here, chin tucked in. We need a half-size really, but we can't have a half-size, so you'll have to have elastic arms. Now, bow like this, in the other hand . . . .'

And then, in Mike's room, we learned that there was another kind of pot-hooks for another kind of language, and books were written in this language too, and Mike knew all about them. Edward sat on the edge of Mike's bed, absorbed, and copied these extended commas, upside-down and right-way up, rows and rows of them, and I was bored and left-out.

'That's what I'd be doing,' said Mike, lying on the bed, hands behind head, 'if jolly old Hitler hadn't mucked things up.'

Mike had been at college, studying music, and would have gone on to do more studying and perhaps be a teacher.

'I don't suppose you've got a piano tucked away somewhere too? No, that would have been too good to be true.'

'Why didn't you want to be a soldier, Mike?' Me, fiddling with Mike's picture of his mother and father, his two sisters, the dog.

'I didn't want to fight people. Kill them.'

'Even if the other person's as wicked as Hitler?' Edward, making treble clefs, intent.

'Even then.'

'Would you if they came here? Fight the Germans?' Me, looking at Mike's books. They have funny names: *Cold Comfort Farm*, *Chrome Yellow*, little thin books with just poems in them.

'I don't know,' said Mike, 'that's what I don't really know.'

'If they were going to kill us and Betty and Pam and Susie?' Edward, completing his treble clefs, moving on to a flourish, a fistful of notes from one of Mike's books. 'Andante,' he copies, in best writing.

'Mmm,' said Mike. 'That's the problem, isn't it?'

'I expect you would, really. Do you mind people calling you conchie?' Me, seeing Betty out of the window. She has been in the kitchen garden, getting vegetables – it must be nearly supper time.

'I'd better not mind, had I?' said Mike.

'Better than getting killed.' Edward, frowning at his blunted pencil, licking the point.

'Right,' said Mike. 'Music class over. That'll be one guinea each, payment in cash only.'

And later, in the playroom, Edward holds the violin again, like Mike showed, and scrapes. It is a dismal sound. It bears little relation to the noise Mike made, and less still to the noises, scrawny but designed, that come from the tulip-mouth of father's gramophone. Something is dreadfully wrong. He tries again, and the scrape is different, and fractionally, marginally more endurable. And he tries again. And again and again and again.

There was harvest, and everyone worked till after it was dark, and Mike had blisters on his hands and walked jerkily, like an old man, from stiffness.

'Breaking you in, then, are they?' said Sandy, complacent, but Betty let Mike have more than his ration of hot water for baths, and there was trouble with Pam and Susie. Pam painted a red line on the bath and no one was to go above it, everyone to be on their honour. Sandy threatened to come up and look through the keyhole, and there was much to-and-fro with the girls across the kitchen table. Mike never joined in this, but he would grin hugely, enjoying it.

And the year slid, somehow, into winter. The hot, harvest, blackberry days were gone and we were into November: white skies, dark spiny trees, hot toast for tea, cold hands, feet, noses. Darkness as we feed the chickens, the stable drive pale-fringed with grasses, the landscape huddled under a violet sky, the fields peppered with snow that fell this morning and melted too soon to be any use to us. Winter mud creeping over paths and up through grass. Birds spraying from the dark and wintry hedges.

'I like Mike. I like Mike next best to Sandy. No, equal best.'

'And Tom Dixon?'

We thought about this, anxiously.

'Equal best to Sandy and Tom Dixon. And Betty,' said Edward.

'When she's not cross.'

Edward, chewing grasses, said, 'I think Mike's brave.'

'Brave?'

'It's brave doing something different from what everyone thinks you ought to do. He doesn't like it when they call him conchie – he pretends he doesn't mind, but he does.'

Collect more poetry, prose and drama extracts to add variety to your final selection.

Consider possible ways of working with the literature, setting your own assignments for talk, writing and drama.

Stage Five

Organisation of material

One suggested title for presentation

↓

Remember, Remember

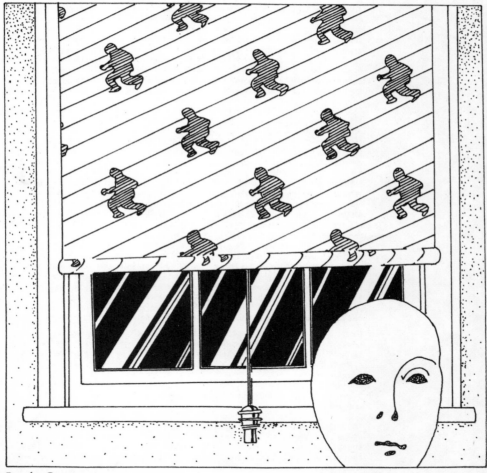

Run for Cover

Acknowledgements

The author and publishers wish to thank the following who have kindly given permission for the use of copyright material:

George Allen and Unwin Ltd. for 'Note to the Hurrying Man' by Brian Patten (1969); Alison and Busby Ltd. for 'Gunpowder Plot' by Vernon Scannell from *Selected Poems*; Amber Lane Press for extract from 'Killed July 1916' (1982) c.Belgrade Theatre in Education; Associated Book Publishers Ltd. for extract from *The Birthday Party* by Harold Pinter, Methuen (1972) c.Pinter (1959); The Bodley Head Ltd. for extract from *Maria Marten* by Montague Slater (1928); David Boulton for 'The Conchies' from *Objection Overruled*, MacGibbon and Kee (1966); Jonathan Cape Ltd. for extract from *Roots* by Arnold Wesker from *The Wesker Trilogy*, and the estate of Robert Frost for 'The Death of the Hired Man' from *The Poetry of Robert Frost* ed Edward C Latham with extracts from Commentary by Louis Untermeyer from *Come In and Other Poems*, and the estate of C Day Lewis and The Hogarth Press for 'The Album' by C Day Lewis from *Collected Poems* (1954); Carcanet Press Ltd. for 'The Suspect' by Edwin Morgan c. from *Poems of Thirty Years* (1982); William Collins Sons & Co Ltd for extract from *Red Shift* by Alan Garner (1973); Curtis Brown Ltd for extract from *The Devil by the Sea* by Nina Bawden c.(1957) and extract from *The Queen and His Rebels* by Ugo Betti (1957); English Centre for 'An Interview with Robert Cormier' from *The English Magazine*; Faber and Faber Ltd. for 'The Evacuees' by Norman Nicholson from *Five Rivers*; Samuel French Ltd. for extract from *Hobson's Choice* by Harold Brighouse c. (1916); Victor Gollancz Ltd. for extract from *After the First Death* by Robert Cormier (1979); Elaine Greene Ltd. for extracts from *The Crucible* by Arthur Miller c. (1952, 1953); The Guardian for review of Ted Hughes *What is the Truth?*; A M Heath & Co Ltd. and the estate of Sonia Brownell Orwell for extracts from *Animal Farm* by George Orwell, Secker and Warburg Ltd. (1945); William Heinemann Ltd. for extract from *To Kill a Mockingbird* by Harper Lee (1960), for 'Studies in the Park' from *Games at Twilight* by Anita Desai (1978), and for extract from *Going Back* by Penelope Lively (1975); David Higham Associates Ltd. for 'The Ballard of Charlotte Dymond' by Charles Causley, Rupert Hart Davis (1961), and 'My Grandmother' by Elizabeth Jennings from *Collected Poems*, Macmillan (1967); Daniel Hoffman for 'The Centre of Attention' from *Able was I Ere I saw Elba*, Hutchinson (1977); Michael Imison Playwrights Ltd. for extract from *The Children's Crusade* by Paul Thompson (1975); William Kimber & Co Ltd. for 'A Wartime Childhood' from *London Morning* by Valerie Avery (1964) and Arnold Wheaton; Brian Marriner for article 'Dreadful Murder on Bodmin Moor—The Charlotte Dymond Murder Case' from *True Crime* (August 1984); The Observer for review of 'The Change-over' by Margaret Mahy; Geraldine O'Donnell for 'The Stone' from *To Be a Writer: A Course in Creative Writing* by Adit Mason, John Murray (1970); A D Peters & Co Ltd. for extract from 'The Skylight' from *Saturday Lunch with the Brownings* by Penelope Mortimer; Laurence Pollinger Ltd. and the estate of Mrs Frieda Lawrence Ravagli for 'Discord in Childhood' by D H Lawrence from Collected Poems Vol 1, Heinemann (1964); Routledge and Kegan Paul Ltd. for 'How to Read a Poem' by Richard Exton from 'The Language of Literature' in *Eccentric Propositions* ed Jane Miller (1984); G T Sassoon for 'The Hero' by Siegfried Sassoon from *The Turning World* ed D J Brindley, Schofield and Sims; Times Newspapers Ltd. for 'Thirty Six Things to do with a Poem' by Geoff Fox and Brian Merrick, *Times Educational Supplement* (20.2.81), and article 'Murder of Charlotte Dymond', *The Times* (1.5.44); Harvey Unna and Stephen Durbridge Ltd. for extract from *The Long and The Short and The Tall* by Willis Hall, Heinemann Educational Books Ltd.

The author and publishers wish to acknowledge the following photograph sources:

Page 4 Victor Gollancz Ltd; Page 5 Macmillan Education/Philip Hood; Page 41 The Louvre/Bazille; Page 42 The Piccadilly Gallery/Eric Holt; Page 45 Haags Gemeentemuseum/Escher; Page 111 University of Bristol Theatre Collection/Angus McBean; Page 145 Rex Features; Page 175 John Topham Picture Library.

The publishers have made every effort to trace the copyright holders, but where they have failed to do so they will be pleased to make the necessary arrangements at the first opportunity.

The authors also wish to thank Jan Martin, not only for typing, but caring about their manuscript; Peter Wyatt, actor, for his letter reproduced in 'Picking up clues'; Steve Leach, for his contribution to 'Centre of attention'; Jo Bryant, for setting *Charlotte Dymond* to a guitar accompaniment and all their colleagues and students in the teaching and learning profession.